INDIAN CASES IN B2B MARKETING

Specially written for the students of

B- Schools across the world

Dr. Dilip M. Sarwate

VISHWAKARMA
PUBLICATIONS
VP

INDIAN CASES IN B2B MARKETING

First Edition - January 2016

© Author

ISBN - 978-81-927132-7-4

Published by:
Vishwakarma Publications
283, Budhwar Peth, Near City Post,
Pune- 411 002.
Phone No: (020) 24448989 / 20261157
Email: info@vpindia.co.in
Website: www.vpindia.co.in

Cover Design
Meghnad Deodhar- Vishwakarma Publications

Typeset and Layout
Chaitali Nachnekar - Vishwakarma Publications

Printed at

Repro India Limited, Mumbai

This book is dedicated to Mr. Anil P. Kumar, MD CTR Manufacturing Industries Limited for the effective use of 'Case Method' in Vision Meets/ training programs.

When I joined the B-School way back in 1969, Marketing was just Marketing. The prefixes to the word were yet to be added. I had never imagined in my wildest dreams that I would enter academics and later will become a writer of several books in management.

I started teaching Marketing in October 1972. Even at that stage, different schools of Marketing were yet to emerge. I was in management consulting based in Pune and my exposure was more to engineering Industries as there were very few FMCG companies. Even though, the basic principles of Marketing remained same; it was obvious that there was a need to develop different schools. Sometime around 1976, two schools in Marketing emerged. They were consumer marketing and industrial marketing respectively. We had to wait almost till perhaps 1985 before the third school namely services marketing emerged. Soon it was noticed that the contribution of Services had already crossed 50% in our GDP!

Now in 2015 when I am writing this Preface, I notice that the era of Mass Marketing is over and it has given rise to Niche Marketing. In most of the MBA programs across the country, the curriculum in marketing has several new prefixes been added. They include rural, international, retail, insurance, banking, agri and many others.

I have also made my modest contribution in this area. In 1989 Loksabha elections, I was advising a national level political party. This gave rise to the pioneering book in the world named **Political Marketing- The Indian Experience** (Published by Tata McGraw Hill). Being entrepreneurial, I produced a Marathi film in 2010 named **Mani Mangalsutra.** This resulted in writing a book on Film Marketing with title **Cinema Pahawa Kadhun!**

When I started teaching marketing, the pedagogy used was only through lectures. Till that time, the Case Method was yet to become popular in India. When I started using Case Method, I noticed a lacuna. There were no cases written till then on Indian situations. We used to borrow cases from IIM (Ahmadabad) who in turn were getting their cases from Harvard Business School (HBS). We had to pay a certain royalty for using these cases. Most of our students could not relate to these cases because they found the environments and the situations given in the cases foreign to them.

I worked with Kirloskar Consultants Ltd. from June 1. 1972 to June 30, 1975. During this time, I had worked on some 160 consulting assignments. I decided to convert this experience in writing cases on Indian situations. Most of the cases were real ones. I had to change the names in most of the cases and also add some imagination to make them interesting. Looking at the interest and patience (?) of Indian students, I decided to keep the length of these cases limited to 5-6 printed pages. As against these, the cases from HBS normally used to be of 20-30 pages!

With little modesty, I can say that my first book

Indian Cases in Marketing Management published in August 1978 was the pioneering book in India on the subject. At those times, a leading advertising professional in India used to write a column Advertising & Marketing under the pen name of Zachary in Economic Times (ET). He had regretted in his column that there is no case book available on Indian situations. My book had just come out and I sent a copy to him. Promptly, he did a book review in ET of almost full page. Can you imagine the power of a book review? I received order for 500 copies within a week from all over India! I am happy to mention that this book is now in 16 th edition. Every edition seeing deletion of few old cases and addition of new and topical cases.

The book reviewer Zachary had made a funny observation at the end. He had said that "he enjoyed the book even though he is not a student of management anymore, the Author should add solutions at the end of the book in the subsequent editions." I had to send another letter to him saying that Case Method is not Arithmetic in which at the end, correct solutions are given. If this is done, it will curb the creativity of students for there cannot be a single solution in Case Method.

I had also sent a copy of my book to Professor Philip Kotler at Kellog Business School (North Western University), Chicago. His reply praising my efforts is still on my file, something to feel proud about!

And then there was no looking back. My consulting experience of now over 42 years gave me enough material to write cases. By now, I have written close to 400 cases, all on Indian organizations, on subjects like market research, marketing communications, entrepreneurship development, strategic management, on excellent companies as well as failed & closed companies. I do not know whether there is any entry on writing of Cases in Management in Guinness World Book of Records! I have found out that the Case Method is one of the most effective learning tools in B-Schools. However, this requires adequate homework on the part of both students and faculty which is lacking.

Presently, in many courses in Marketing, a specialization under B2B Marketing is offered. There are good text books available on the subject both by foreign and Indian authors. However, once again, there is a paucity of cases on B2Bmarketing. I am trying to bridge the gap with this book.

I have been advising a B2B company in Pune with a wide product mix since 2007. In their Vision Meet, which is held twice in a year to accommodate all managers, since last four meets, I have used case method. The origin of some of the cases in this book goes to my esteemed client for which I am thankful to them. I hope that this book too will be received well. Your feedback is always welcome.

November 15, 2015

Dilip M. Sarwate

Professor Emeritus IGI

CONTENTS

Section One
Introduction

Basic Concepts of B2B Marketing

What is happening on marketing front?

Adam Smith in his famous book Wealth of Nations written in 17 the century had told us that the primary business of any business is to remain in business. He, however, did not tell us how to do this. Now in twenty first century, the answer is obvious. You can remain in business only if you get customers and can succeed in retaining them.

The job of getting customers and retaining them is done by the discipline of Marketing. In a business organization, there are different disciplines like R & D, Production, Purchase, Finance, HR and others. All functions are equal but no one can deny that marketing is the first amongst equal. For it generates revenue for the organization while all others result only in expenditures!

What are the latest happenings on marketing front?

- **Marketing is becoming all pervasive:** There is no organization on earth which does not require marketing. Earlier, it was thought to be of use only for profit making organizations. However, now non-profit (NGOs), small & large, private as well as government organizations and everyone needs to market themselves to fulfill the organizational objectives.

- **Environments at global, macro & micro level changing:** The environments all around us are rapidly changing. They are on account of economy, technology, public policy and culture. They pose both threats and opportunities. This is typically described as turbulent times. An organization has to take quick and purposely actions to overcome the threats and to grab the opportunities. Marketing plays a major role in this.

- **Customers are becoming demanding:** Gone are the days when an organization could tell their customers take it or leave it. Not only customers are demanding, they have the law on their side. The Consumer Protection Act 1986 has given considerable power to the buyers against those of the sellers. No organization can afford to ignore the forces of consumerism.

- **Competition is becoming fiercer:** In India, up until 1984, most of the organizations enjoyed a monopoly. They exploited the customers by offering sub-standard products & services, never bothered about after sales services and developing new products. The broad banding policy introduced by Rajiv Gandhi in 1984 and later the liberalization in 1991 changed the picture completely. Newer players came in the market offering better products & services. It has become a matter of survival of the fittest. Al Ries & Jack Trout defined modern marketing as a civilized form of warfare. Now the marketers are facing global competition. The organizations now will have to come out with strategies to outsmart and outmaneuver the competition.

- **Technology is rapidly changing:** There is no guarantee against technological obsolescence. Theodore Levitt had said that if it is not your own technology which can make your product obsolete, it could be someone else's, anywhere in the world. The invention of microprocessor chip in the early eighties and the internet in nineties completely revolutionized marketing. A new prefix makes virtual marketing a different ball game both for product and services marketing. The laptops, smart phones in hardware and latest software's, data mining & warehousing, cloud computing are the buzz words in today's marketing.

- **Marketing costs are on the rise:** In a seller's market, the expenditure on marketing was minimal. Aiming to attract more customers and to cope to competition, organizations have increased their budgets on marketing and its sub-functions like market research, marketing communication and logistics. The cost of marketing has gone up to 40% of the income, particularly for FMCG companies.

- **Marketing is becoming social:** Marketing is certainly not all about generating profits. Majority of the organizations admit that it has a social angle. Thus, social marketing, societal marketing and social cause marketing have become a necessity to survive in the business.

What is marketing?

American Marketing association offers over 52 definitions of the word marketing. This shows how different people perceive marketing. However, one definition to understand the meaning will suffice.

Marketing is a process of exchanges to satisfy needs & wants to generate customer satisfaction and fulfilling the organizational objectives.

Type of exchanges

- **B2B:** In the mid seventies, this was typically called Industrial Marketing. However, the nomenclature used presently is B2B marketing. This is the exchange taking place between the producers to producers and/or resellers. This could be for original equipments, components and/or for industrial services. The typical buyers were end users, jobbers and/or middlemen dealing in these lines. The major objective of the exchange is profit. Sell of products like a diesel engine, castings & forgings, heat treatment services and alike will fall under this category.

- **B2C:** This was typically called earlier as consumer marketing or what also was termed as FMCG marketing. The exchange is taking place between the producer to consumers and customers. The buying objectives are mainly to satisfy the individual and family needs of physiology, psychology, social and self-actualization needs.

- **C2C:** There is a huge market for used items. This may include products like books, apparels, automobiles and thousand other products. But how will consumers exchange with consumers? This was made possible through technology and advent of internet. One of the pioneering company who set up their business under this heading in the world was undoubtedly ebay.com. Today, many more have come out through their portals to provide this facility. In India, indiatimes. com, quickr for products and naukari.com, shaadi. com for services respectively are few examples who have become very popular.

- **C2B:** Few organizations who would like to be more customer friendly are using this exchange process. This could be for customer relationship management (CRM), complaint handling, obtaining customer feedback, new product idea generation and many more. Two MNC's like Proctor & Gamble and HP are famous for using this avenue. Every year, they receive thousands of hits.

There are few more terminologies which are put to use. They include C2M (Consultancy to management), C2G (Consumer to government) and so on. The basic idea is to have a two way communication involving obtaining feedback from the customers.

What is Marketing Management?

- **Analyzing marketing opportunities:** The primary job of any business is to look for opportunities. They could be in local, regional, national and in international markets. They could be in different demographics or with different end users.

7

- **Researching and selecting target markets:** A study of different markets become necessary to define target markets which look most attractive at this moment. This may be called market research leading now to market intelligence. This is the exercise of data collection through primary and/or secondary research from customers, suppliers, dealers and others.

- **Understanding customer expectations:** Marketing as a discipline has evolved over the years. It has gone through the stages of product concept, production concept, selling concept to the present age marketing concept. It then becomes imperative to study the buyer behavior and to understand their expectations of attributes. The organization then can design its offer to meet customer expectations.

- **Competitive positioning:** There is no business on earth which has no competition. The latter coming from similar & substitute products, coming from organized and/or unorganized sector and from domestic to overseas suppliers. The objective then becomes offerings which are competitively superior and as perceived by the customers.

- **Designing marketing strategies:** Once the target markets are identified and customer expectations are studied, then it is matter of designing the marketing strategies. These are the decision variables to fulfill the marketing objectives. They could be short term and/or long term as the case may be.

- **Planning marketing programs:** These are the time bound activities which are carried out by the organizations to achieve their goals.

- **Organizing, implementing and controlling marketing efforts:** In order to achieve the objectives, an organization needs to create a marketing organization defining hierarchy, authorities and accountabilities. The plan and the strategies will have to be implemented and monitored to bring the targets and achievements as close as possible.

Marketing as a Function

Is there really a function called Marketing in an organization? One can argue that there are several sub-functions of marketing in the department. They are

Briefly discussed below:

- **Marketing research/market Inelligence/competitive intelligence:** Market Research is an exercise in data collection, analysis of this data, drawing conclusions and offering recommendations on any marketing problems. They may include launch of new products, understanding consumer behavior, study on competitors, measuring customer satisfaction and so on. Today, from simple market research, the discipline has moved to market intelligence and competitive intelligence. An organization can decide to have an in-house MR department or can decide to avail services from consulting organizations.

- **Marketing communication:** Marketing communication is required to create awareness, comprehension building, to establish legitimacy, for lead generation and many others. The communication tools available are advertising, public relations and sales promotion. A choice of different media like print, audio, audio-visual, post, outdoor and now digital is available. Again, an organization can set up an in-house department for this function and can also avail of services of external agencies. The advent of social media like Face book, Twitter, Linked In and others are changing marketing processes in every field.

- **Sales management:** There is no organization on earth which does not require salespersons. The job of salespersons is prospecting, communicating, handling objections and closing the sale. The success of an organization largely depends on the effectiveness of the sales force.

- **Market logistics:** All decisions from place of production to place of consumption are covered under this heading. It will include decisions on order processing, inventory control, warehousing, transportation and more.

- **Service:** In a competitive market where all products have started looking identical and are at almost same prices, it is the service element in marketing which will give a competitive advantage to an organization. It will include both before sales and after sales services.

- **Marketing administration:** This will include such areas as marketing planning & strategy formulation, target monitoring, training and others.

- **Marketing finance:** It is a general accusation against marketing executives that they are more target oriented and ignore the profitability aspects. They will have to understand the financial implications of marketing decisions. This will include close monitoring of credit and discount policies, turnover of finished goods and inventory control, managing of debtors and others.

- **Marketing innovation:** Innovation has been defined as something which is perceived by the customers. Hence, it is not mere R & D but marketing R &D which will be needed. Marketing Executives thereby playing a major role.

B2B Marketing

We have discussed the basics of marketing so far. This will be relevant to any type of marketing. Let us now try to go deeper in B2B marketing which was earlier termed as Industrial Marketing.

Def. Marketing of products and services to commercial enterprises, government and other profit institutions either for resell to other industrial consumers or for use in the production of their own products or services.

Classification

- **Entering goods:** This will include right from basic raw materials like steel, aluminum and other metals, components like castings & forgings, machined components, fabricated parts and others.

- **Original equipments:** These are the finished products which will include different types of machineries, equipments like diesel engines, pump sets, electrical motors, commercial vehicles, tractors and so on.

- **Facilitating goods & services:** These will include packaging & forwarding services, transportation, heat treatment, installation & erection services, general insurance and many others.

- **Engineering projects:** Project marketing is gaining ground as against product marketing. Instead of just selling a product, if an organization can offer a total project, typically termed as turnkey services, it can generate more revenues for the organization. This is called services from concept to commissioning. The customer is also benefitted as they do not have to chase several vendors and the project can be completed in time as well as within budgets.

Difference between B2B & B2C

It will be necessary to understand the differences between the two major markets in the world, notably the industrial markets and the consumer markets respectively. This difference will decide the strategies and decisions to be taken for the two markets.

The difference in the two markets can be understood on following basis:

- **No. of customers:** The number of customers in B2B markets could be as small as one and seldom goes beyond few thousands, For example, an organization like Hindustan Aeronautical Limited (HAL) may have only one customer, that is Indian Air force, for a company manufacturing CNC Controlled Vertical Turret Lathe, the potential customers in the country could be hardly 40-50 numbers in a year and for all types of pumps (agricultural & industrial) the number may go to 6 lakhs in a year. As against that, theoretically, the consumer market in India for consumer goods & services will be of the order of 1210 million, that is the population of India. This will have repercussions on all marketing decision variables that include product, price, place and promotion.

- **Geographical concentration:** It is obvious that consumer markets are spread across the country while industrial markets are concentrated in certain geographical pockets. For example, most of the mining sector is concentrated in eastern sector, textile industry is in western zone, IT sector is concentrated in five towns of Bangalore, Mumbai, Chennai, Hyderabad and Pune respectively and so on. This will have an impact on market logistics decisions.

- **Non homogeneity:** The industrial buying will depend on the size of the organization, their production capacities, terms & conditions and so on. A giant like Tata Motors requires pig iron in very large volume and an engineering ancillary industry also requires pig iron in a small volume cannot be comparable. This will give rise to differential pricing. As against this, in consumer markets, in a certain demographic profile all customers are expected to behave in the same manner. Hence, the price of the goods will be same.

- **Derived demand:** The demand for industrial goods is mostly dependent on extraneous factors like economy, technology and government policies. That is why this sector is more vulnerable to threats like recession, obsolescence and government expenditures. Hence, the demand is dependent on many factors on which the organizations may not have any control. As against this, the demand for consumer goods is dependent on population growth and disposable income. As such, organizations in consumer marketing with the help of adequate marketing efforts can influence the demand.

- **Buying objectives:** The buying objectives in B2B marketing mostly is profit oriented if not profiteering. As such, technical and commercial aspects play a major role. In consumer markets, the buyers buy the products to fulfill their personal needs & wants. As per Maslow's hierarchy of needs, a customer first buys to satisfy his physiological needs of hunger, clothing & shelter. Then he buys to meet his psychological need of beliefs, security & others. Next are the social needs of belongingness, esteem & pride. Finally, he goes to satisfy his self actualization needs. A study of buying objectives influences in designing marketing communication, positioning and others.

- **Buying operations:** The buying operations in B2B are routine. The organizations have a list of approved vendors to whom the enquiries are sent. Occasionally, tenders are advertised in media and proposals invited. First, they are evaluated on technical grounds and then on commercial grounds of price, delivery, discount and credit terms. Negotiations always take place. As against this, consumer buying operations take place when the needs are felt. Typically, there is a pre-purchase activity of window shopping, evaluation of alternatives, fulfillment of attributes expectations, actual buying, use and then there is considerable importance given to post purchase analysis. The last one is called cognitive dissonance!

- **Buying organization:** In B2B marketing buying organizations are well defined. It may involve R & D department on technical matters, purchase department on commercial matters, production department on operational matters and so on. As against this, in consumer buying, there is nothing like a formal organization. However family members, neighbors, relatives and brand ambassadors play the buying roles of initiator, influencer, decider, purchaser and finally the user. This helps in defining the target markets and communication strategy.

- **Competition:** In B2B marketing, there are few players from organized sector and there could be large number of manufacturers from unorganized sector. The latter offers the goods at lower prices which large manufacturers cannot offer due to their higher overheads. However, the quality could be suspect. In consumer marketing, there are few players in large scale manufacturing having their presence across India. There could be small players, mostly imitators, catering to local & regional markets.

Expectations of Industrial Buyers

The actual research of industrial buyers gives an interesting picture of their expectations and priorities.

15

This is because the industrial products are critical, of high value and invariably require after sales services. The buyers would not like to take risks.

Given below is the list of expectations and the hierarchy in industrial buying.

- **Technical & Delivery capability:** The buyer would like to ascertain that the supplier has proven technical capabilities which can be vouched by satisfied customers. Delivery is also a key aspect in determining the supplier.

- **Consistent quality:** It is important that the supplier is known for maintaining consistency in quality. A buyer would like to be convinced about the quality policy used by the manufacturer.

- **Competitive pricing:** Contrary to the belief, all industrial buyers do not necessarily buy the cheapest products. Also negotiation is an accepted fact in B2B marketing.

- **Repair services:** Industrial products regularly require periodic maintenance as well as spare parts. Easy availability of this is given considerable weightages by buyers.

- **Performance history:** Referrals of existing users and a satisfactory report by them is of considerable importance. These testimonials can help in convincing a new buyer.

- **Production facilities:** The buyers may like to visit the shop floor of the manufacturer to find out the quality of facilities available with them. This will include plant layout, availability of modern machinery, quality control measures put to use and others.

- **Brand image:** The buyers do not only buy products. They buy the attributes & benefits provided by the manufacturer. They look for brands which can satisfy their ego requirements.

- **Financial position:** Many discerning buyers will do a credit rating check of the supplier that they are financially in a position to give delivery on placing the order as per the contract. This mainly includes availability of working capital for production. A delay can result in opportunity costs.

- **Management philosophy:** Ultimately, an organization is known from its management philosophy, value systems, importance given to maintaining quality and other such social factors. Developed countries would refrain from buying if they find child labor is employed.

Understanding the B2B Markets

All types of markets are brought on a common platform using the concept of 7 O's of markets as shown below:

7 O's of Markets

- **Objects:** What does the market buy represented by a customer? This will include the range of products, equipments and services. An organization accordingly can go for strategy on product differentiation.

- **Objectives:** Why does the market buy? What are

their preferences in terms of technical capabilities, delivery, price and any other aspects?

- **Organization:** What is the organization structure of the buyers? How much emphasis is given by each department? And so on.

- **Operations:** How does the market buy? What processes and procedures are used by them?

- **Occupants:** Who are the actual decision makers?

- **Occasions:** When does the market buy? Is there a pattern or seasonality seen?

- **Outlets:** From where does the market buy? Does it buy directly from producers or buys from resellers?

As can be seen, answers to these questions can provide guidelines to the marketers to design their strategies.

4 Ps (Marketing Decision Variables)

The 7 O's of markets give rise to 4 P's of marketing mix.

- **Product mix:** Type of products, sizes, specifications, materials of construction, packaging and any others. This is a decision in product differentiation which is a key to marketing success.

- **Price mix:** Basic prices, duties & taxes, discounts and credit period.

- **Place mix:** Location of plants, warehousing, mode of transportation, inventory levels, direct versus indirect marketing, selection of channel members.

- **Promotion mix:** Advertising, publicity, sales promotion, personal selling, media planning and positioning.

Marketing Planning & Strategy Formulation

Every organization will have to plan for their future. This will require setting objectives and designing strategies to fulfill them.

This includes the following:

- **Setting of objectives:** Specific, measurable, attainable, relevant, time bound (SMART).

- **Designing strategies:** These are the decision variables which could be short and long term respectively to achieve the goals and targets.

- **Formulation of policies:** These are the rules & regulation, the framework in which the organization operates. The policies need not be rigid and depending on the circumstances can be kept flexible.

- **Action plan:** These are the operations which are carried out in a time bound manner. A year can be divided in four quarters, goals & targets are set and the performance is monitored.

- **Monitoring & control:** A regular review to ensure that the performance and the targets are as close as possible. Similarly, the expenses are close to the budgeted amounts.

Strategy Statement

The strategy statement for any organization is defined under following heads.

- **Target market definition:** Where should the organization focus? The choice being in domestic or overseas markets, for the former in zones & regions, for latter the specific countries. In B2B marketing, the target markets are mostly defined in terms of end users, their locations, volumes they procure and their preferences.

- **Product differentiation:** This is the range an organization would like to offer in terms of product lines, product types, specifications, sizes, materials of constructions and so on. In B2B marketing, many times it also includes the auxiliary products on optional basis to make a system/project.

- **Pricing:** The pricing strategies include from basis prices, duties & taxes, transportation charges depending on the mode of transportation used, discounts offered which could be for a certain volume for a single order or for a rate contract spread over a year, credit period, installation charges and so on.

- **Distribution:** These are the strategies which include all decisions right from the place of production to place of consumption. They include inventory decisions, mode of transport, warehousing, installation and any others which can give the organization a competitive advantage.

- **APSP:** These are the strategies organization use to

communicate with their different types of customers. This will include the effective use of the promo tools like advertising, publicity and sales promotion. For B2B marketing, sales promotion like technical manuals, seminars, participation in trade fairs, demonstrations have been found to be more effective, Under publicity, newsletters and press releases are mostly used. The advertising is mostly restricted to technical magazines.

- **Services strategy:** The B2B products invariably require both before sales and after sales services. In the former, help in selection of correct product, offering guarantees for performance and helping in raising finance are often used to win customers. For the latter assistance in installation & commissioning, warrantee against manufacturing defects, periodic maintenance and supply of spares promptly are desired by the customers.

- **Positioning:** Positioning is creating an image in the minds of the customers as against a competing product. In B2B marketing, positioning is mostly done with respect to product specifications, benefits assured, targeting to a customer group and against a major rival. It is basically a communication strategy which involves message design and media planning.

- **Sales force:** This is the strategy used by the organization to decide the right quantity and quality of their sales force, compensation plan, incentives and others.

- **Market intelligence:** In today's marketing warfare, this discipline has become very necessary. The information on competitors & customers will have to be compiled on every aspect to take decisions to outsmart the former and win the latter.

- **Marketing innovation:** Customer demands are insatiable. They want something new every time. The B2B organizations will have to invest in a discipline like value engineering to continuously improve the product and try to reduce the costs. They must improve on technology continuously.

- **Marketing budgeting:** A certain budget needs to be allocated to marketing. as a percentage of income, for B2B companies. It normally ranges between 5-7% of income (as compared to 35-40% for B2C companies). A major portion is allotted to field selling followed by logistic & APSP.

Marketing Control

All successful organizations world over show a common pattern. That, they are very good in controlling the marketing efforts.

It is done under following heads:

- **Annual plan control:** This includes sales analysis, market share analysis, marketing expense analysis and financial analysis. It periodically monitors the targets and achievements. Readymade software's are also available for this purpose. This can help in increasing the marketing efforts or taking any other strategic decisions.

- **Profitability control:** This analyzes profitability by product types, sizes & materials, territory, customer, segment, order size and any other basis. This helps in developing a mix which can result in optimal performance.

- **Efficiency control:** This evaluates the efficiency of sales force, advertising, sales promotion, and dealers. Certain norms can be set aside for each of these entities in marketing operations. The actual performance can be measured and improvements can be suggested.

- **Strategic control:** In today's modern marketing practices, this includes marketing effectiveness rating instrument, marketing audit, marketing excellence review, company's ethical and social responsibility review, measuring customer retention and satisfaction surveys and so on.

Today, the above activities go under the name of Business Analytics and readymade as well as custom built software's are available.

Summary

For every market, the answers to following questions will provide directions:

- Who is the target customer of our products?

- Where are they located? What are their expectations?

- How big is the market? At what rate it is growing?

- Who is the competitor? What are their strengths & weaknesses?

- How to outsmart and out maneuver the competitor?

- How to retain and satisfy the customers?

- How much to spend on marketing? How to earn adequate profits?

The Case Method

What is a case?

A case is the description of an organization at a certain period of time, containing its history, its external environments and internal operations. It exposes issues, problems and aspirations at that particular juncture.

The Cases written are always real. They are built around a theme and expanded to make them interesting. However, from a legal point of view, most of the times, the names of the organizations as well as the persons are changed

Objectives of case method

The Case Method is a learning tool used mostly in the B-Schools and Law Schools. The main objectives of using this pedagogy are as follows:

- **Acquire skills to apply concepts to practices:** A considerable amount of theory is taught in B-Schools which include tools & techniques, models and so on. All these can be applied to do analysis of a case given.

- Develop habits of compilation of facts, diagnosing problems, Analysis, evaluating alternatives and formulating workable plans: It is not that all the data related to the case is given. Purposely, some data could be kept missing. The case method teaches compilation of relevant data both from primary & secondary sources. It develops analytical abilities. It teaches that decisions are not made on information but on the options available. Finally, it requires developing plans which are feasible.

- **Self learning:** The text books can teach concepts. The case method teaches applications of the same.

- **Exposure to different types of organizations and different types of problems:** The problems given in a case study could be unique. They may include different sectors, size of organizations, types of organizations from manufacturing, trading, services and others as well as in different disciplines like marketing, finance, HR and others. In a span of 2 years in a B-School, a student can be exposed to some 100 and more situations of different nature. In his entire career, it is unlikely that he will get an exposure of this kind.

- **Developing team work:** It is recommended that a case should be studied in a team. This can generate a synergy and team spirit.

- **Focused approach:** Most of the cases have typical problems. It develops the ability of students to quickly pinpoint the same.

- **Zero risks:** The case method is a class room work. The suggestions made are only hypothetical. As they are not necessarily to be implemented as well as do not require actual expenditures, they carry zero risks.

- **Career planning:** With exposure to different types of industries and the problems faced by them, a student can identify his liking and aptitude which can help him to chalk out his career path.

Benefits of case method

Following benefits accrue through case method:

- It makes students think clearly

- It helps them devise creative action plans

- They can use different quantitative tools while doing case analysis.

- One of the most important benefit is to know the importance of information

- If the case analysis is to be presented verbally, it improves communication skills of students.

- If it is to be given in written form, it teaches students to write clear, forceful and convincing reports

Limitations of case method

There are few shortcomings of this method. They are as follows:

- The cases can become outdated. For example, a case written in early 70's on Typewriters will have no relevance today with the advent of word processors.

- The Balance Sheet given, say for the year that ended in 2009, may not be of much use in 2015, because six more years have passed and the latest Balance

Sheet will now be available. It is not possible to keep on updating the cases.

- It requires some domain knowledge of the industry it covers. For example, there is a case on CNC Controlled Vertical Turret Lathe which is priced in excess of Rs.40 lakhs. If the students do not know the product and its target customers, they may come out with wrong recommendations like advertising on TV!

- The secondary data on the industry covered may not be available easily. If available, there could be ambiguities in the same. In that case, the students tend to base their arguments only on the data given in the case. This could be inadequate.

The case method is supposed to be a group work. However, it has been seen that only few members may do the work and others may remain silent spectators. This will defeat the purpose of case method of learning.

Guidelines for Case Analysis

There are no hard & fast rules on case analysis. Given below are some general guidelines:

- Read the case given to you carefully. First, hurriedly and later carefully making notes of the important issues covered.

- Carry out a situational analysis of both internal and external environments. This may be covered under the headings of economy, technology, public policy and culture for macro environments. The internal environments can be studied under leadership qualities, R & D, production facilities, marketing, finance, HR and others.

- Identify the problem area/s. There may be one or several problems the organization might be facing.

- Analyze the reasons for this situation and why it happened. Whether the causes were controllable or non-controllable?

- Use various concepts, tools & techniques to analyze. This can throw a good light on the situation.

- Evaluate the various options available for the problems under study. They may include the worst like closure or dynamic like expansion and growth.

- Amongst the various options under consideration, recommend the one which you consider the best under the circumstances.

- Recommend a time bound action plan and who will execute it. What external help could be needed?

- Do secondary research and compile macro level data relevant to the industry and the organization. From Google Search, collect information on product, applications and if possible quantitative data on market demand, import/export statistics, market share of leading players and so on. This will help you in developing competitive strategy.

Tools used in Case Analysis

There are large number of tools available for case analysis. They are all part of management innovations which have been developed by different thinkers over last 150 years. Only a partial list is given below. Students are advised to get more details from the relevant text books. (Recommended reading: Management Innovation –Strategic Tools for Decision Making by Dr. Dilip M.Sarwate)

Strategic Management

- SWOT analysis
- BCG product portfolio matrix

- Mckinsey 7-S frame work
- GE market attractiveness model
- Porter's model on competitive advantage of nations
- Porter's model on competitive strategy
- Balanced score card
- Blue ocean strategy

Marketing

- Sales analysis
- Market share analysis
- Marketing expense analysis- use of marketing ratios
- Attitudinal tracking & Consumer behavior theories
- Product life cycle

Finance

- Financial ratio analysis
- Inter firm comparison
- Investment appraisal techniques (ROI, Payback period, DCF/NPV)
- Break even analysis
- Sensitivity analysis
- Variance analysis
- p/e analysis

Behavioral Sciences

- Theory X and theory Y

- Theory Z

- Theory U

- Maslow's hierarchy of needs

- Herzberg's motivational theory

- Managerial grid

- Intrapreneuring

- Situational leadership

Details on each tool can be obtained by referring to a right text book.

Section Two
Cases in B2B Marketing

(All the cases are real. In some cases, the names have been changed)

Karlekar Brothers Limited (KBL)

Business Planning

The Managing Director of KBL was delivering his opening speech at the annual planning meeting that was being held at Hotel Taj Aguada Fort in Goa. There were some 25 persons who were present for this 3 day meet. They included the heads of department of all functional areas and also their Vice President (Corporate Planning).

"We should all be concerned about the future because that is where we are going to spend the rest of our lives. All successful companies world over show a common pattern that they are very strong on their long term planning. We have done well so far but I think that we have become complacent. We have not given adequate attention to planning for the future. In next three days, I would like you to brainstorm on what new products we are going to launch in next 5 years, which new markets we plan to enter and all related aspects of production, finance, HR and everything else."

The MD, Dhananjay Karlekar had set the ball rolling. He had clearly spelt out the theme of this meeting. It was now up to the participants to do the needful.

The History

KBL was set up by Laxmanrao Karlekar exactly 100 years back at a barren place called Karlekarwadi in Sangli district, some 220 kms from Pune. Laxmanrao was earlier a drawing teacher but he was fired with entrepreneurial ambitions. He managed to get some 100 acres of land from the then King of Aundh- Pant Pratinidhi. He started manufacturing centrifugal pumps for agricultural use. The real growth of KBL came under the leadership of Shantanu Karlekar, MIT (USA) trained son of Laxmanrao. Dhananjay represents the fourth generation of Karlekars.

Karlekar group grew over the period and set up some 28 independent Companies manufacturing diesel engines, electrical motors, transformers, machine tools, castings and many others. All were separate legal entities. The philosophy of the company was very clear- 'We are engineers first and hence we will only grow in engineering field'.

Besides pumps, KBL also manufactures different types of industrial valves. They also have a factory in Dewas (MP) which manufactures Agriculture Pumps. At Karlekarwadi, they manufacture variety of industrial pumps and valves. They consider themselves as Leaders in India for Fluid Handling.

Financial Performance

Some of the salient features of the organization are given below:

The present turnover of the company is around Rs.1600

crores. Approximately, 50 per cent of business comes from exports to some 60 countries in the world.

The company made a net profit of Rs. 30 crores year ended March 31, 2012.

The present contribution of business is given below,

- Pumps   40%
- Valves   10%
- Turn key projects   50%

Market share for agriculture pumps in India is around 20% and for industrial pumps is around 50% thereby making them market leaders with 35% overall market share.

The share price of KBL for a face value of Rs.10/- is being quoted on the Stock Market at Rs. 160/-

Marketing Mix

The marketing mix of the organization can be described as given below:

Product Mix: KBL makes 20 types of pumps, in 30 different sizes, in 6 materials of construction thereby offering some 3600 combinations of pumps. Such a wide range is necessary to meet the specific requirements of different segments of the market. The materials of construction are decided on the basis of the characteristics of the fluid to be handled. Presently, they are only making Centrifugal Pumps and they have not given any thoughts to manufacture Positive Displacement Pumps.

The range of valves similarly is very large available in different materials of construction. Typically, with every pump, minimum two valves are needed, one for inlet and another for outlet.

Price Mix: KBL are cost leaders. Their prices of agriculture pumps are almost 100% more than similar pumps offered by unorganized sector. There are close to 400 manufacturers of agriculture pumps in the country. When it comes to industrial pumps, the competition is between some 10-15 leading manufacturers where KBL has to be competitive. One of their major competitor is the German company KSB Pumps based in Pune.

Place mix: KBL has close to 140 dealers across the country as well as in some 40 countries abroad. The dealers are given 10% discount and 30 days credit as a general policy. In addition, they are given incentives in the form of volume discount, cash payment, on target achievement and so on. The best dealers every year are also given attractive prizes in cash or kind. Those dealers who reach the targets are taken on holidays to exotic locations like Bangkok, Singapore, Mauritius and so on.

Promotion mix: KBL is in B2B business. They spend approximately 0.5% of their income on APSP. This includes occasional advertisements in national English Newspapers and regular advertisements in technical journals devoted to pumps. For Publicity purpose, they come out with a news letter called Cascade six times a year which now goes to some 5000 readers. In Sales Promotion, they have the best documentation on pumps & valves in the country. This includes product brochures, technical manuals, performance charts, trouble shooting, spare parts manual, price list and delivery schedules. A separate price list is available for overseas markets. They periodically participate in engineering trade fairs held in India and abroad.

SWOT Analysis

The pump market worldwide is booming. There is no industry in the world which does not require a pump of some kind or the other. KBL pumps have a good reputation in the market.

KBL has several strengths. They are,

- A wide range meeting the requirements of almost every type of end user.

- An elaborate R & D set up at their works.

- The best hydraulic research laboratory in the country.

- A brand equity being in the business for last 100 years.

However, there are certain weaknesses which they have to overcome. They include,

- A high R & D cost resulting in higher prices resulting in lost orders.

- Long delivery period resulting in lost orders

- Poaching of their sales engineers by rivals. KBL hires engineers from good colleges and gives them one year of exhaustive training. On an average, 50% of them quit and join the major competitors at higher salaries within two years. This is one of the worry of management.

Aspirations

KBL aspires to become the largest manufacturer of pumps in the world by 2020. It is not merely a pipe dream. They realize that this can be achieved only through long term planning and establishing strategic alliances Worldwide.

With such a large product mix, their major problem is in demand forecasting. They cater to 25 major segments of industry which includes water supply power generation, chemicals, mining, textiles, paper, fire fighting and others. While the company overall is enjoying a growth of almost 12% per annum, it is becoming difficult to predict from what segment the orders will come and for what type of pumps. This is also putting restraint on production planning as well as procurement. Almost 50% components are bought out items. Another area of concern is low profitability. Almost 50% of their business comes from government sector which creates problem of receivables. The recovery erodes profitability

Give your suggestions how they should plan their future to become the Indian MNC. What are the different management tools they should put to use? How they should restructure their organization and so on?

Durocrete Testing Laboratory - Growth Strategy

Leading management consultant Dr. Dilip Raju was invited by Durocrete Testing Laboratories Private Limited (Durocrete) for consultations. It was divided under two heads. The first half was for training to the sales & marketing staff and the second half of the day with top management to chalk out growth strategy.

Micro Level

The first half of the program was titled Art of Selling& Handling Objections.

There were 30 participants in the program which included few back office staff other than the sales team. Raju asked the sales team to list out all possible objections they have encountered while doing duty for Durocrete. He put on the board a list of all these objections. The major ones included,

1. Our rates are more than the competitors.

2. Most of the customers are demanding longer credit period while the management focuses on faster recovery.

3. Most of the customers ask for a higher discount on our prices.

4. The customers complain that it is very difficult to reach your office as they find the telephone numbers mostly busy.

5. Sometimes the test reports are not delivered on time as per the promise.

6. Few others

The discussion then started on how to overcome these objections? He made a pertinent point that if you do not close a sale, you will remain only as communicators and not sales persons. I want to create live wire salespersons from you!.

Problems of Sales & Marketing Team

Most of the members in the sales team are young (Below 25). They are diploma holders or graduates in commerce, civil engineering or in management. They are selected through newspaper advertisements. After initial training, they are allotted a certain territory and client list. They are given a target of around 25 customers to meet every week of which at least 30% have to be the new ones. Besides order booking, they also have to chase the clients for recoveries. A separate marketing executive is appointed to follow-up for recoveries beyond 90 days.

Not all the members in sales team achieve their targets. Either they quit on their own or they are asked to quit. The attrition rate is as high as 30% every year which increases the cost of recruitment & training.

The marketing executives, as they are called, are offered incentives on a quarterly basis on achieving the targets.

The sales team meets weekly on every Monday with VP (Marketing) for target monitoring and monthly with MD and other senior staff and discusses their performance. It is heartening to note that the morale of the sales staff is high. Concluded Raju in his training program, "I would like you to place Importance on Relationship Marketing in the backdrop of a demanding customer and growing competition. Remember, that customer retention is more important than customer satisfaction"

The History

Durocrete has completed 12 years of its operations on March 2012. It was started by Mr. Ujwal Joshi (39) in Pune in the garage of his father's bungalow on University Road. Ujwal did his B.E. in Civil Engineering from MIT on Paud Road, Pune. Later, he did MBA from SIBM, Pune. He worked for a year with a consulting organization and got some experience in Market Research.

Ujwal always wanted to be on his own. In his market research assignments, he was looking for opportunities. The civil construction activity for residential as well as commercial operations in Pune was booming. That is when he thought of starting a Testing Laboratory for civil construction. He started with an investment of little over Rs.50,000/-. Now, he operates from rented premises of around 4500 sq. ft. on Sinhgad Road, Pune where he has a full fledged laboratory. Durocrete is a private limited company of family members.

Durocrete opened its second laboratory in Nasik in 2008 and the latest one in Trombay (Mumbai) in November

2011. Today, he has testing equipments worth over Rs.500 lakhs in these three centers.

The present manpower is Pune (75), Nasik (10) and Mumbai (15) which include staff in marketing, operations, administration and accounting.

Service Mix

Durocrete offers following testing services to end users which include Builders, Architects and Project Management Consultants.

- Cube testing for cement
- Steel testing
- Non Destructive Testing
- Soil Testing
- Pile Testing
- Chemicals testing

The last three services have been started only one year back and show a good promise. The first three services contribute equally at 30% and the last three contribute 10% of the total turnover. For the chemical testing, the company has invested in a Spectrometer costing Rs.20 lakhs.

New Services

Following new services could be explored:

a. Wind Tunnel Testing for tall buildings – Approximate investment needed will be Rs. 1crore. Metro towns mainly will be the markets.

b. **Pile Dynamic Testing** – Approximate investment needed will be Rs.50 lakhs. Again, metro towns will have to be explored.

If these services are launched, Durocrete could be only the second such Laboratory in the country. However, there is no assurance on Return on Investments (ROI)!

Pune Market

As per the data compiled by Pune Builder's Association (Called CREDAI), there are approximately 3000 builders in Pune & Pimpri-Chinchwad. They are categorized as follows:

Large builders: Those who build more than 5 lakh sq. ft. per year of civil construction. Their number has been estimated at around 50.

Medium scale builders: Those who build from 1 lakh up to 5 lakh sq. ft. per year. Their number has been estimated at around 200.

Small builders: Those who build less than 1 lakh sq. ft. per year. Their number is estimated to be around 2750.

Customer Mix

The sales target for March 31, 2014 was Rs. 8 crores which the company achieved easily registering a YOY growth of almost 30%. The PAT was at 7% of the turnover. As per the data painstakingly analyzed by the VP (Finance), they have a present customer base of

1200 in the three markets catered by them. The sales contribution shows the following picture based on ABC analysis,

A type customers giving annual business of Rs 5 lakhs and more- 60 numbers

B type customers giving annual business of Rs 1 lakh but less than Rs 5 lakhs per annum - 200 numbers

C type customers giving annual business less than Rs. 1 lakh - 940 numbers

Market Potential

Presently, Durocrete is only concentrating on builders. However, a great potential exists from various projects which typically come under the name of Infrastructure projects. They include building of highways, bridges, flyovers, dams, factories, power stations and many others. Unfortunately, on many of these projects, quality is not given much importance. One such area is the Roads of Pune. The jokes are being cracked whether there are potholes in the road or roads in the potholes. The issue is politicized. However, the major problem is the use of sub-standard raw materials. Hence, it is believed that if these raw materials are tested by a reputed laboratory and then they are put to use, some of the problems could be minimized.

By a rough estimate, the market potential for Pune is estimated at Rs.15 crores per annum for civil testing services. As such, the potential is much larger that what Durocrete is in a position to manage presently.

Approximately, the market potential in Mumbai Metropolitan Region is 4-5 times bigger than Pune. However, the competition is also fierce. Besides private laboratories, similar testing facilities are also offered by engineering colleges and government's testing laboratories.

The sales team was feeling that business was reaching saturation levels and the company needed to enter new testing segments and markets to achieve further growth. Construction testing business was a sunrise sector especially with more than 500 billion$ investment expected in the country in infrastructure segment in next 5 years alone. This would naturally boost construction testing business. The business was growing albeit at slower pace than expected due to slow down in the real estate.

The target

Based on the earlier growth, Durocrete became ambitious and set a target for FY 2014-15 of Rupees 10 crores. The expected contribution from the 3 Centre's was as follows:

- Pune   Rs. 7 crores
- Nasik   Rs. 1 crores
- Mumbai Rs. 2 crores

By the end of third quarter (December 31, 2014), the company had achieved the target of Rs. Rs.4.5 crores only. Both Nasik and Mumbai were way below the targets.

Problems

Durocrete has established a good brand image in Pune market where they enjoy a market share of almost 40%. At Nasik, they have a market share of around 50%. The Mumbai market has still to be tapped fully and presently they are using market penetration strategy.

Some of the strengths that Durocrete had are as follows. These can be called their USP:

a. Prompt service

b. Accuracy of test results

c. Very strong technical team

d. NABL accreditation

e. In house developed ERP to manage laboratory business

f. Introduced and pioneered the system for collecting samples from site.

However, their near monopoly in Pune is now shattered. They are competing with six more laboratories in Pune, four in Nasik and almost 25 in Mumbai who are offering similar testing services. The new entrants are quoting lower rates and offering more credit period. The major problems faced by Durocrete are as follows:

- Every quarter, they find that they are losing customers to their rivals. Loss of one A type customer means loss of revenue of almost 1%.

- The receivables are rising. Presently, it is 90 days

which erodes their profit. Every year, they have to write off around Rs. 5 lakhs as bad debts.

- The logistic costs are on the rise with increase in the price of petrol & diesel.

- Many unscrupulous clients insist on getting reports which are favorable to them. Since inception, Durocrete believed in ethical practices by refusing to give manipulated reports. This has also resulted in losing some business.

National Accreditation Board for Testing and Calibration Laboratories (NABL)

All prestigious clients insist on having an accreditation from NABL This gives them a confidence in testing results. For almost 10 years since inception, Durocrete had not bothered to go for this recognition. However, they realized that it is a must for establishing a brand equity. They started the process sometime in April 2012. It is a long drawn process which requires spending few lakh rupees. Now they have got recognition for Pune laboratory and for Mumbai it is pending. This is likely to give them a competitive advantage and an edge in the market.

Organizational Conflicts

There is no organization on earth which does not have any conflicts. Durocrete is no exception.

Ujwal Joshi is the MD of the company. Under him, there are three Vice Presidents. They are Vishwas Kale (43) Vice President Operations, Suneel Deshpande (42),

Vice President Marketing and Amol Kulkarni (38) Vice President Finance.

When the organization was small, they all worked very closely like a family. The growth in its wake brought conflicts.

The nature of conflicts is as follows:

- Marketing blames operations for delays in completing the tests. The promises made by marketing team are not honored and they get the flak from the clients. Occasionally, the reports sent to the clients are with errors. Sometimes, reports of one client are sent to another.

- Operations team blames the marketing team for not giving clear instructions, last minute changes made in the specifications and lack of feedback from clients.

- The conflict between marketing versus finance is the routine observed in every organization. That includes giving indiscriminate discounts without consulting finance, problems of recoveries and in quite a few cases writing them as bad debts resulting in losses. Even though the Mumbai operations are new, the promise made by marketing head that the break even will be one year looks to be far too away.

It is then left to MD to sort out the differences between the three main functional heads.

Macro Level

Growth strategy

A brain storming session was started in the afternoon by Dr. Raju for the top management team of Durocrete. It was decided to plan for next 5 years which included opening laboratories in following towns:

- Delhi
- Ahmadabad
- Nagpur
- Bangalore
- Hyderabad

Following points emerged from the discussions:

a. The investment needed to start a new centre was about Rs. 1 crore.

b. Major decisions to be taken are whether to give priority to putting new laboratories or add new testing services

The young MD is ambitious and hopes to set up around 15 similar laboratories across the country in next 10 years. He has not given much thought how he is going to achieve this. There are three options available to him. They are,

a. Set up all laboratories on his own. This will require substantial funds for real estate, testing equipments towards fixed assets and working capital towards salaries and other day to day expenses. How should these funds be raised? What are the options that can be considered? (Organic growth)

b. Setting up joint ventures in all these places identifying the persons/organizations that would be willing to invest in equity. The questions which need to be addressed are as follows:

- Should they look for people who are associated with construction industry in one way or the other? Or they can consider others also?

- What should be the equity sharing?

c. Develop a model of franchisee that will make all the investments in starting the laboratory in their town. Durocrete will give technical knowhow and training to run the Lab. For this, they will charge a down payment and a royalty on sales every year. The enterprise management will be the responsibility of the franchisee. The company had tried franchising approach in Mumbai. However, it did not get adequate response.

The punch line of Durocrete is **Test with the Best.** What recommendations you would offer to the company? The brief financials are given in appendix

Appendix

Brief Financials of Durocrete for last 5 years

Sr. No	Particulars	FY 2007-08	FY 2008-09	FY 2009-10	FY 2010-11	FY 2011-12
1	Revenues (Sales)	195.09	213.27	205.43	302.08	471.9
	(YTY Changes in Sale)					
			9%	-4%	47%	56%
2	EBITDA	53.83	55.536	39.94	60.43	70.62
	EBITDA is-earnings before interest, tax, amortization and depreciation and dividing it by the company's total amounts of revenue.					
	(YTY Changes in EBITDA)		3%	-28%	51%	17%
3	EBITDA%	27.59	26.04	19.44	20.00	14.97
	% WITH REVENUE					
4	EBIT	44.68	42.99	29.57	44.84	56.76
	Calculated as revenue minus expenses, excluding tax and interest					
	(YTY Changes in EBIT)					
5	EBIT%	22.90	20.16	14.39	16.17	12.03
	% WITH REVENUE					
6	EBT	39.12	34.42	22.37	45.55	54.91
	Revenue- Expenses (excluding tax)					
	(YTY Changes in EBT)		-12%	-35%	104%	21%
7	EBT%	20.05	16.14	10.89	15.08	11.64
	%WITH REVENUE					
8	EAT (PAT)	27.36	21.81	15.08	30.36	37.65
	Net profit earned by the company after deducting all expenses like interest, depreciation and tax					
	(YTY Changes in EAT)		-20%	-31%	103%	23%
9	EAT (PAT)%	14.02	10.23	7.34	10.14	7.98
	%WITH REVENUE					
10	Current Ratio Business Liquidity	1.90	1.39	1.76	1.55	1.86
	CA / [CL=cl& provisions+CC+US.Loan)					

Regaining the Leadership Position - Case of Radiators

It is said in USA, when you reach number one position, there is only one way you could go- that is down. Should this be applicable to business organizations? The answer is a 'No'. However, if that happens, something is amiss. It could be lack of consistency in marketing efforts, technological obsolescence or superior competition. What went wrong for RTC?

The history

RTC was started in 1968 to manufacture Radiators and Flange Mounted Tap Changers in Pune. As such, they were pioneers in the manufacturing of Radiators in India. They had developed good clientele in first ten years. For some financial setback, RTC was acquired by the leading electrical equipment manufacturer Crompton–Greaves (CG) and became its subsidiary. The installed capacity of RTC was just enough to meet the captive requirements of CG and they lost track of other customers.

In 1995, RTC again became an independent legal entity. They decided to reduce their dependence on CG. However, by then, it was late. They found it difficult to penetrate the market and lost their leadership position. With addition of different product lines like Tap changers, Transformer Explosion Prevention System and others, Radiators was put on the back burner. Its slide for RTC continued.

Product description

RTC had obtained the technical knowhow to manufacture radiators from world leader, German company named Menke Incorporated. The radiators are used with oil filled transformers. Transformers are of three types,

Distribution transformers up to 5 MVA Medium size industrial transformers from 5 to 25 MVA Large power transformers from 25 to 350 MVA

For strange reasons, the capacity for manufacturing radiators is expressed in terms of sq. meters (sq. mtrs) and not in terms of numbers or weight. RTC had created a capacity of 110,000 sq. mtrs to begin with.

Technical aspects

The user and manufacturer industry both had a limited technical knowledge of the product. Over the years, improvements had to be made. It was expected that the product will be leak proof. Some other technical improvements were as follows:

- The external painting which earlier was 7 tank process was changed to shot blasting process because many paint related problems arose.

- Change over from seam welding to spot welding

- Top customers like Tata Power demanded spray galvanizing and special paints like Poly Urethane resulting in cost increase by almost 50%.

- Aesthetics is another area which requires substantial improvements.

It is strange but as of today there is no Indian Standards (IS) for radiators. As RTC got its technology from Germany, they were following DIN Standards. It requires a thickness sheet of 1.5 mm while in India most of the radiator manufacturers are offering 1 mm thickness sheet. This creates problems in aesthetics. The unorganized sector manufacturers of radiators do compromises with thickness to match prices. The earlier machine tools available with RTC had their limitations.

Now RTC has installed latest Roll Forming machinery imported from Turkey which will be able to overcome the earlier limitations.

The average life of a radiator is from 20-25 years.

The competition

For first ten years or so, RTC were market leaders and enjoyed a share of around 70% and more. By 1995, there were 4 major manufacturers of radiators. Barring RTC, all others were in unorganized sector, mostly proprietary organizations. Today in 2015, the market share of RTC has slumped to 3%.

The major players with the share of market are as follows:

TTP (Bangalore) Market Leader   40%

HiTech (Thane)	20%
PE (Hyderabad)	15%
20 other manufacturers	22%

The market is growing approximately at 10% per annum.

Competitive advantage of RTC

The advantages and disadvantages of RTC can be highlighted as given below:

Advantages

- RTC is the only supplier of radiators from organized sector.

- Transportation economics makes RTC most suitable supplier for Western Zone where major OEM's are located.

- RTC with its global presence can tap export markets. This, however, requires hot dipped galvanized radiators. This will require additional investment of around Rs. 4 crores in equipments.

Disadvantages

Due to higher overheads, RTC prices are about 5-8 % higher than their major competitors. These can only be absorbed if much higher volumes are generated. RTC was virtually absent from the market for number of years.

Target customers

Almost all the business of radiators comes from transformer manufacturers. There are around 200 transformer manufacturers in India. They contribute

almost 98% business of radiators. The balance 2% coming for replacement from utility companies like State Electricity Boards, NTPC and so on. As such, the radiator manufacturers have to meet the expectations of transformer manufacturers and have to be on their approved vendors list.

The ABC analysis shows the following picture:

Class of Transformer Manufacturers

Approximate Numbers

Class of Transformer Manufacturers	Approximate Numbers
A class (CG, Siemens, ABB, Areva)	10
B class	40
C class	150

The registration & approval processes of A type of customers are quite elaborate and meticulous. They are also time consuming. RTC has already started the process and have successfully obtained approval from CG. The cost of radiators is approximately 3-4% of the cost of transformers.

The financials

The present installed capacity for radiators available with RTC is of the order of 5 lakh sq. mtrs. The present capacity utilization is of the order of 120,000 sq. mtrs. As per present calculations, the break even capacity has been estimated at 180, 000 sq. mtrs. The present contribution of radiators in the revenue of RTC has dropped down to 7% from 100% when the company started its operations.

The future

RTC will have to seek answers to several questions if they want to make an impact in the market for radiators. These include,

- Why and how did they lose their number one position in the market for radiators?

- What lessons have been learnt?

- What should be the strategy to penetrate the market, achieve break even quickly and aim at capturing 22% market share by 2017?

- What strategies they must adopt to increase exports of radiators? To which countries they should target and why?

- What other strategic options they should exercise?

Finally, RTC aims at regaining their leadership for radiators. The question is how?

Marketing Planning & Strategy Formulation for Petroleum Fire System

Breaking News

A major fire at the terminal of Indian Oil Corporation at Jaipur destroys the entire terminal. 16 lives have been lost and the monetary loss has been estimated at Rs.400 crores. Government will be setting an inquiry to investigate the cause of fire and what future preventive measures should be taken to avoid such repetitions.

Like many other breaking news on TV channels every minute, this news also will be forgotten by majority of the population. However, those who know the complexity of the problem will understand its seriousness.

Thousands of fires happen across the country throughout the year. To extinguish them, we require efficient fire prevention systems. Petroleum products are most hazardous. The system required to prevent fire while handling them, has to be highly efficient which will come in to service within seconds. Such systems have to perform mainly two tasks viz fire detection and fire extinction respectively.

Are there any such systems available?

Rim Seal Fire Protection System

Saval BV from Netherland has developed a system which can meet the expectations of the industry. They have installed close to 5000 systems worldwide. It is heartening to note that this system is available to RTC for marketing in India. A formal MOU has been signed with them.

The CFI system as it is named, for protection of rim seals on floating roof tanks is a fully fabricated system. It uses CF3I (a liquefied fire extinguishing agent, super pressurized with Nitrogen). In case of fire, its heat will cause one or more glass bulb detectors/sprayers to open and the CFI extinguishing gas will be released by the detector/ sprayer directly into the fire. The CFI storage container is equipped with a pressure & level switch which will send an alarm signal to the control panel once the CFI has been released from the container. Enclosed product literature will give more technical information on the system.

Advantages

This system offers number of advantages. The main ones are given below:

- Very fast knockdown of the fire (within 2 seconds)
- Only system immune to effects of lightning
- Reliable glass bulb sprinkler detection technology
- No manual intervention is required
- Very low maintenance required

As such, this technology should have a great potential in India as well as anywhere in the world.

Market scenario in India

The number of customers for this system could be small. However, considering the price and the utility, it holds a great potential. Presently, there are 6 major potential customers. They are,

Public sector

- Indian Oil Corporation (8 Refineries, 236 tanks)
- Hindustan Petroleum (4 Refineries, 59 tanks)
- Bharat Petroleum (2 Refineries, 47 tanks)
- Oil & Natural Gas Commission
- MRPL

Private sector

- Reliance Petro
- Essar Oil

The system can also be fitted on all terminals. All put together, it has been estimated that the potential for these systems is of the order of 800 numbers. The prices for the system range from Rs 20 lakhs to Rs 100 lakhs, depending on the diameter of the tank. The potential for this system can be gauged from this data.

After the Jaipur fire, Government of India set up an inquiry committee under the Chairmanship of Mr. M. B. Lal, Ex-Chairman of HPCL. The committee has given clear recommendations that all petroleum tanks must be fitted with fire prevention systems.

It has been estimated that the annual requirements for these fire systems in India could be of the order of Rs. 1600 crores per annum. Export potential could also be substantial.

Competitive scenario

After identifying this technology, RTC, an engineering company prepared Indian Standards (IS) for this system. It was approved by Engineers India Limited (EIL). When Firewall was on the verge of making a major breakthrough in this line, a competitor named Vimal Fire emerged on the scene. It is not yet established whether it was through their political clout or some other influencing methods, they made changes in the specifications suiting their system. It had certain shortcomings besides being 10-25% costlier than Firewall. It was found out that they could not fulfill one statutory requirement.

A third party also approached to provide system for fire prevention but could not meet the approvals needed.

The Petroleum Ministry has floated a tender for Rs.300 crores to procure Rim Seal Fire Protection System. RTC has to come out with strategy to get this order in full or split with other supplier?

Government Markets

What is a government market?

Barrona Marketing Directory from USA defines government market as,

Consumer group composed of central, state, and local government units. The government market in total accounts for the greatest volume of purchases of any consumer group in the United States, spending hundreds of billions of dollars on goods and services each year. Although government purchases comprise a wide range of products such as food, military equipment, office supplies, buildings, clothing, and vehicles, selling to this market typically involves a great deal of paperwork, financial constraints, bureaucratic barriers, and awareness of specific political sensitivities.

Major segments of government markets in India

When we think of government markets, it will have to be sub-segmented on the following lines:

Central Government: This comprises of various ministries and the purchases made by them. The Central Government prepares five year plans and decides the allocations on various ministries. Presently, we are at the fag end of eleventh five year plan. The draft of the 12 th five year plan is under preparation and all organizations will have to study it to find out what allocations will be made for ministries who are their possible customers. In addition, every year in February the annual budget is announced with allocations and fiscal policies. No wonder, annual budget is watched and studied carefully by the industry and business community.

State Governments: We have now 29 states and 6 union territories. They have their own sources of revenues in addition to allocations made by the Central Government. On the basis of the same, the State Governments prepare their own annual budgets.

Local governments: These are at Municipal Corporations, Municipal Councils, Zilla Parishads and Gram Panchayat levels. Each one of them have their budgetary allocations from which procurement of goods and services are done. Some of these markets could be very big like Mumbai Municipal Corporation whose annual budget is of the order of Rs.25,000 crores while that of Pune is also in excess of Rs. 8500 crores.

Public Sector Undertakings: One can argue whether it is the business of government to be in business. However, the fact is that there are large number of Public Sector Undertakings (PSU) both at Central as well as State levels. At Central government level, some of them like NTPC, EIL, ONGC, IOC and many others could be major customers of RTC. At state level, if we only consider Maharashtra State, then organizations like Maha Generation, Maha Transmission and Maha Distribution are the major customers of RTC.

It will be seen that to cater to this market, the suppliers will have to deal with both the beauracracy as well as the polity. To handle them together could pose certain problems which will have to be overcome.

In every country, the government is the biggest customer as well as biggest marketer. It is truer in India. It becomes imperative to understand the business processes while marketing to this sector. The tendering procedure, lobbying and in all honesty, the kickbacks cannot be overlooked. It is not necessary that the best technology and lowest prices, not necessarily together, will be acceptable. At the same time, the great potential offered by this sector cannot also be ignored.

RTC will have to come up with all possible strategies to capture this potential. More importantly, they will have to develop the right positioning strategy. The aspect of Ethics also cannot be ignored. Should they pay heed to the saying that Good ethics leads to good business?

Concept Testing for Diagnostic Products

"There is no guarantee against technological obsolescence, if it is not your own technology which can make your products obsolete, it could be someone else's, anywhere in the world" were the prophetic words of Theodore Levitt, Professor of Marketing at Harvard Business School in his legendary article Marketing Myopia published sometime in 1964. The words are relevant today also in 2015. On the contrary, in a fast changing technology with reduced cycle time, they are crucial.

What is a concept?

It is a part of Innovation. It follows the cycle of Ideation- Invention- Innovation- Adaptation in that sequence. Innovation is something which is perceived by customer as something which is new.

New product decisions normally take the following route:

- Idea generation
- Screening
- Concept testing
- Feasibility study

- Product development
- Test marketing
- Commercialization

Diagnostic products for transformers

In an electrical power system, transformer is one of the costliest instruments. Particularly, for a sub-station, the cost of a transformer could go in few crores. Experience shows that the failure in a transformer normally happens at the level of Tap changers and/or at Bushings. The problems are mainly mechanical due to wear & tear.

The prices of tap changers may range between Rs.3 to 15 lakhs. However, a failure at tap changer may result in major damage to transformers. Industry, therefore, has been demanding a product which can prevent the failure of tap changer.

On load tap changer analyzer

Yensol (Canada) introduced this product in the year 1987. Since then, it has been popularly marketed in Canada and China. The other major markets like USA, Europe and Latin American countries took time to adopt it. In India, it could still be a novelty.

Specifications

An on load tap changer operates several times a day to provide precise voltage according to network load without interrupting the service. It is therefore important to maintain the on load tap changers. The Yensol analyzer operates on the principle of Vibro Acoustics. The potential of this diagnosis has been recognized by IEEE and CIGRE, the agencies which offer recognition for electrical equipments. The technology of TAP 4 has been validated on many types of transformers over last 15 years.

Tap 4 reveals a wide variety of mechanical and electrical problems viz. contact wear, drive & synchronization problems, arcing in diverter & selector, brake failure, abnormal arcing, coking, misaligned contacts, loose contacts and contact bounce. As can be seen, the list of problem identification is long. By installing this Analyzer on the on-line tap changer, diagnosis results are obtained in less than 15 minutes.

The benefits

- Can be used on any types of tap changers

- On line operation and short testing time

- Robust, light and portable with ability to sustain damage due to accidental drop of voltage

- Easy installation of Analyzer and Current Sensor

- Can be used in high voltage environments

- At present, there is no similar or substitute product available in the market

In developing new technologies, organizations have to spend substantially on R & D. This product is also not an exception. Most of the organizations, therefore, resort to market skimming pricing. The price of Yensol Analyzers in Indian Rupees works out to around Rs.25

lakhs. This is almost 100% more than the price of a tap changer. The question is, will the Indian Industry buy this product at this price? One more limitation is that it can only diagnose the problem but it cannot rectify the same automatically!

RTC thinks that in a longer run this product may have a great potential in Indian markets. RTC are leaders in manufacturing tap changers in India. They have also started exploring international markets which also look bright. This product thereby fits in their core competency.

RTC will have to seek answers to several questions before they decide to market this concept in India. Some of these questions are,

- Should they get a market research (MR) done to test the acceptability of this concept?

- Who should do this MR? Should it be done in-house or should they engage a professional agency for this work?

- How much they should spend on MR?

- After the findings of MR, how should they develop Marketing Strategy?

Can you provide some guidelines to them?

Marketing Mix for Safety Paints

Hindustan Times, Kolkata, December 9, 2011: Eighty-nine people choked to death, many of them in their sleep — some too ill even to move — at Kolkata's posh AMRI Hospital early Friday morning when thick smoke from a fire in the basement of the hospital spread through the central AC ducting and engulfed the seven floors. The scale of tragedy dwarfed the 1997 Uphaar Cinema fire in Delhi (which killed 59) and the 2010 Stephen Court fire in Kolkata (which killed 43).

Incidentally, this was the second fire at AMRI. The previous one, three years ago, had not resulted in any deaths. West Bengal chief minister Mamata Banerjee, who also holds the health portfolio, cancelled the license of AMRI, one of eastern India's leading private hospitals. She has ordered a probe into the fire. And by evening, the Kolkata Police arrested six of the hospital's directors – including RS Goenka, who is also co-promoter of FMCG major Emami, and SK Todi, also promoter of real estate and financial services group Shrachi – who surrendered before the authorities.

Though the cause of the fire has not yet been ascertained, Gopal Bhattacharjee, director of the fire department, said it was most likely the result of an electrical short circuit in the basement car park, which was being used illegally as a store for combustible material like LPG cylinders, engine oil, PVC pipes, bedding, etc. Kolkata Police said in the evening that it had asked the hospital to vacate the store in July.

"The fire didn't spread at all and was confined to the basement. But the thick black smoke went up through the AC ducts and spread through the entire building," he said, adding: "The mechanism to stop smoke from spreading didn't work."

The news item as above is the recurring phenomena across the globe. The fire results in loss of lives as well as property.

Why is that fire safety products and systems are woefully inadequate to curb such tragedies? Wait till you hear of a new technology which now will be available in Indian markets and can help in minimizing such accidents.

Safety Paint Products

SVT Germany has developed what are being called as Safety Paint products. The fields of applications and technical details are given below:

Fields of application

Intumescent fire protection coating on water based dispersion for indoor use. Approved product for cable, pipe or combined penetration sealing's as well as for joint seals and special components (concrete protection). Product is furthermore used as protective coating for cables and cable support structures in dry areas to prevent a fire spread caused by short circuit or external fire source.

Reaction to fire classification

B2 according to DIN 4102-1

Features

Solvent-free and non halogen.

Handling

- Product needs to be stirred Well.

- Application possible with brush, paint roller, or airless spraying machine.

For spraying method

Nozzle orifice > 0,019 inch = 0,48 mm). Mixing with max.2 % water.

Storage

- Protect the product from frost

- Cool and dry (+5°C up to +25°C)

- Shelf life at least 18 months.

Safety instructions

PYRO-SAFE FLAMMOPLAST KS 1 is a non-hazardous material according to the German Gef Stoff V regulation and a non-dangerous according to GGVS/ADR.

Hindustan Chemicals (HC) feels that this product can have excellent Market potential looking at the recurring fires taking place. However, they will have to do a systematic market research to assess the feasibility of launching this product. These are a range of multiple products under the name of safety products. They include,

- Fire safety coatings for cables, conduits and others.

- Fire stop barriers called electrical windows which can prevent fire at the point of a switch-fuse unit or a circuit breaker.

Target customers

It will be interesting to find out who could be the target customers for this product. Presently, following segments have been identified. But, the real customers may emerge differently.

- Real estate owners including shopping malls

- Utility area of petroleum companies, steel plants

- Interlock keys for petroleum and/or gas valves operator safety product

- Any others

Competitive scenario

It is not that this is a unique product and the markets do not know about it. There are at least five competitors in category a) as above which includes big

74

names like 3M & Stanvac and in b) category, there is a Swedish company. The Swedish company is the global leader with 60% market share. SVT holds the balance share. There are domestic manufacturers who also offer a substitute product. The prices of domestic manufacturers are at Rs.200/ litre while the prices of foreign makes are above Rs.600/ per litre.

Market size

Presently, there is no information available on the market size of safety paint products. Prima facie it could be large. HC would like to initially do trading in this line and later may think in terms of obtaining the technology to manufacture the products in India.

The questions?

HC will have to study the market with respect to 7 O's of market (Objects, Objectives, Organization, Operations, Outlets, Occupant, and Occasion) on the basis of which they can decide marketing decision variables in terms of 4 P's (Products, Prices, Place and Promotion). Can you be of help?

Pacemaker - Extending the Life of a Transformer

Can a machine or a product be compared with a human being? The answer is 'Yes'. There are many similarities as given below:

- A machine/product as well as a human being has a certain life span.

- Both go through the cycle of Introduction, Growth, Maturity and Decline.

- A machine and a human being can fall sick. Under the circumstances, both require treatment.

- The cost of healthcare is on the rise.

- There are Mediclaim Policies available for human beings. The premiums are also on the rise. What insurance is available for engineering equipments?

- Both have to be maintained properly to increase the life.

In last few years, all over the world, maximum deaths of human beings are on account of cardiac failure. The critical conditions are detected through a series of tests like an ECG, Stress Test and Angiography in that order. The remedy is available through Angioplasty and a By-pass surgery. In many cases, a patient is fitted with a Pacemaker to enhance the life of the heart as well as the human being. Can a similar Pacemaker be developed to enhance the life of costly machines?

Electrical Power Industry

Since the time Benjamin Franklin discovered electrical energy, its need has been ever growing. Electrical power is required for household use as well as for industries. All over the world, alternative sources of energy are being developed. As of today, the major sources of energy are given below:

Hydel power: Water is stored in a dam and is forced at a speed on a turbine which generates energy by rotation. Water is available in abundance and could be the cheapest form of generating electrical power. The capital cost for high capacities could be much higher and may create problem of rehabilitation of population.

Thermal power: The coal is burnt and its energy is used to generate electricity. This is a major sector contributing to energy needs of the nation.

Nuclear power: This is considered as a clean energy. However, there is resistance to setting up of nuclear power stations particularly after the Tsunami tragedy which hit Fujiyama Power station in Japan in 2011.

Natural gas: The natural gas finds world over have given rise to setting up power stations based on this raw material. Dabhol Power station in Konkan is one such example.

Wind power: Wind generators with natural wind can generate electricity.

There are experiments being made to generate electricity by unconventional methods. These include use of agriculture waste like Bagazze which is a by-product in sugar mills. This is called co-generation. Some other alternatives include Ceramic Fuels, diesel power and others. It is important to understand the cost of power generation by each means. Economies of scales are important.

While talking on this subject, it is worthwhile to note the statement made by JRD Tata in 1975 when the country was going through severe power shortage. He had said that there is no power which is costlier than the costliest power. When you want it, you want it at any cost.

Should RTC think of entering the field of energy generation? May be in non-conventional form of energy, setting mini-power stations?

Transformers

Transformer is a major electrical equipment. It is mainly used to step up or step down of voltages. After generation of electricity, it is transmitted through the grid across the nation. This transmission is done underground as well through overhead transmission towers normally at high voltages in excess of 400 KV to bring economies. This power is made available to industry at 440 volts while for residential purposes, it is made available at 230 volts. This step down is done with the help of transformers.

Transformers are required in generation, transmission

and distribution of electricity. The range could be from 33 kv to 1 MV. They may be broadly classified in three types,

- Distribution transformers up to 5 MVA

- Medium size industrial transformers from 5 to 25 MVA

- Large power transformers from 30 to 350 MVA

The large power transformers are of high values. The price range from 30 MVA to 350 MVA could vary from Rs. 3 crore to Rs.36 crores respectively. The typical life span of a transformer would be 25 years. There are close to 200manufacturers of transformers in the country. However, those making power transformers would be around 20 or so in organized sector.

What are common goals of On-line Maintenance of Power Transformers?

The operational short term maintenance is oriented towards quick recovery of the **operational reliability** of the transformer. It usually starts after the detection of a not-permissible deviation from the main parameter(s) of the oil-insulation system, most often the drop of the die-electric strength of the oil. The process primarily focuses on the restoration of the given parameter(s) within the limits required by IEC norm.

The life extending maintenance is focused on the **savings** achieved **by the prolongation of the life-time** of the transformers under **safe operational conditions.** The long-term or even continuous maintenance process is started by the detection of the complex symptoms of the rapid aging of the oil-cellulose system. The process is primarily focused on the reduction of aging process in the cellulose insulants.

VS-06 Pacemaker for a transformer

Enhancing the life of a transformer is done by separating the undesired elements. Water, oxygen and heat are the main enemies of a transformer. Water and hear accelerate the ageing process of paper insulation and produce further water and chemicals thereby reducing the life. VS- 06 is being used as a natural separator of excess water in paper. This helps in minimizing the ageing process.

Oxygen oxidizes metals and non-metals, which in turn create acid and damage oil property. Some transformers do not have moisture breathing but have gas generation problem. Be it combustible of or oxygen, beyond a limit, they reduce the life of a transformer by creating electrical faults. VS-06 is used dedicatedly for degassing in some installations.

This technology is unique and is safe for oil and paper of transformer which neither separates beneficial parts nor stresses paper of transformer. Some of industrial processes (Aluminum/Steel) using smaller plants require no outage. Continuous fitment of VS-06 can avoid this eventuality or accidental outage.

Competitive scenario

Product specifications

This product is manufactured by a Czechoslovakian company named ARS Altamann. The technical process how it works is given below:

The hardware and software gives easy and permanent optimization of the transformer dehydration process. Regardless of how efficient any method of oil dehydration might be - the dehydration of the transformer means water removal from its cellulose materials. Moreover, any on-line transformer dehydrationis ultimately governed by slow diffusion of moisture from cellulose in the oil and this process can be accelerated only by high temperature.

The second basic law of any on-line dehydration is:

high transformer temperature --› high moisture in oil --› high separation, but --› low dielectric strength of oil.

And in order to avoid the lowering the immediate reliability of transformer, we have therefore to tune at least two antagonistic criteria in time-related profile:

- Max. separating efficiency of separator (max. water removal rate)

- Dielectric strength of oil - has to be maintained or improved. This way is possible not only to monitor and optimize the function of the VS- 06 separator but to optimize the whole dehydration process as well, by strictly controlled warming-up of the transformer.

Target customers

This product will have two major segments. They are,

- All end users like utility companies and others who have invested heavily in a transformer and would like to enhance its life.

81

- OEM's (Transformer manufacturers) who would like to offer this as an optional accessory.

There are thousands of installations across the country where this product can be used.

Competitive scenario

A local made product of reverse engineering is available at around Rs. 6 lakhs. Imports from USA and New Zealand at Rs.10 lakhs have been already approved by the Utilities. If RTC decides to market them, they will also have to price it at the same level. At the moment, the potential available in numbers or in Rupee terms has not been estimated.

How to market?

The crucial question will be how to market this product? RTC prices could be of the order of Rs.60 lakhs per unit. This will require convincing the potential customers to accept it. Besides price, positioning will play a major role. As this will be a B2B product, sales promotion will have to be effectively used. What type of sales promotion will be needed will have to be worked out.

Can you suggest marketing strategy for RTC which will bring results?

Inter Departmental Conflicts - Organizational Behavior

ABC Engineers are in the manufacture of Engineering Components required for Automobile Industry for last 35 years. It was January 7, 2013 and the MD had called monthly meeting of all the HOD's to take a review of the performance of first three quarters. The atmosphere was tense as the company had underperformed and had missed the targets by at least 30%.

"The year 2014 was economically bad. The worldwide recession, took a toll of almost all the industries. Particularly, the engineering industry was badly hit. This, however, does not give a justification for our poor performance. This meeting has been called to take a review of the situation and to develop strategies for the last quarter so that we can recover as much ground as possible" were the introductory remarks of the MD. "We have all the HOD's present today and I would like to hear from each one a frank analysis of their performance up until now" saying this, he called the meeting to order.

The VP (Marketing) was always the first to take the initiative.

"The recession indeed has hit the engineering industry badly. However, the Automobile sector, particularly, the passenger car industry, has registered a healthy growth of 15%. We have a good order position but we have failed to deliver. In my frank opinion, I would list out our failure in following areas,

- Our deliveries are getting delayed. As against a commitment of 45 days, we are on an average taking 60 days to deliver. This has resulted in cancellation of many orders.

- The rejection rate which used to be 4-5% has gone up to 7%. The blame thus lies with Production Department in both these areas.

- As many new models of passenger cars are being launched by the OEM's, they are asking for new components with enhanced strength and aesthetics. Our R & D department had made a commitment of lead time of 6 months. However, even after one year, they are yet to deliver components meeting customer requirements. The OEM's have to import these components and we are losing opportunities. I do not know how long they will remain interested in us.

I think it's high time that our Production Department gears up to meet the commitments" concluded VP (Marketing).

The above statement came as a hot blow for all. The VP (Production) was red faced.

"Wait a minute. I would not accept this accusation. VP (Marketing) has painted a picture which is convenient to him. There is another side to the story which he has been ignored. I would like to take his charge point-by-point.

- Ask the marketing department how many times they have changed the specifications in last one year. It takes time to change the jigs & fixtures.

- In many cases, the delivery was ready but the customer did not come for inspection. We followed with marketing department several times but they think that their job is only to get orders and nothing beyond that.

If this results in delay, why should we take the blame" was the justification given by VP (Production).

It was a general impression that there was a substantial rivalry between VP (Marketing) and VP (Production) as they were the two senior most persons in the organization since its inception. Both had a firm opinion that the organization was running only because of their inputs!

VP (Finance) interjected and started speaking, "I would like to point out the serious financial position we are in.

- Our debtors have gone up to 120 days. At the rate of interest @16% pa for working capital, I hope you gentlemen realize how much we are losing by way of interest.

- Normally, we keep an inventory of raw materials for 45 days. However, I find that now it has gone to almost 120 days. This is putting a big load on our limits. I had to ask our bankers' to give us overdraft facility.

Interrupted VP (Materials), " What can we do? There were rumors floating that the Steel prices are likely to go up by

80% and we had no other option but to build inventory at lower prices offered by our vendors for volumes".

"Yes, but the actual price rise was only 15% during this period" Said VP (Finance).

"We also did not get adequate marketing staff. We are short by at least 10 persons to tap the new entrants. HR is taking too much time to select. Our compensation package also is not very attractive. During these nine months, we have lost almost one third of our staff. More seriously, they have joined our competitors. We are today laughed at as a good training institute for our rivals" said VP (Marketing).

"Do not blame me for not being able to attract and retain talent" Said the VP (HR). "This is a matter of policy".

The MD was listening to all this free for all. It was not that this was happening for the first time. It is but natural to play the blame game. The company had enjoyed a steady growth of almost 25% per annum over last 10 years. The situation had become grim only on account of recession and underperformance.

"Does anybody else has to say anything" questioned MD. "I would like to know what will be your KRA's for next 3 months. Can you give them to me in just one line" demanded MD.

VP (Marketing) said, "we will double our marketing efforts to achieve the targets".

VP (Production) said, "we will reduce our cycle time and rate of rejection".

VP (Finance) said, "I will try to curb the expenses by 30%".

VP (HR) said, "No more training programs for the staff, all over time also will be disallowed.

VP (Materials) said, "We will reduce the inventory to 45 days".

Is there any organization on Earth where there are no conflicts? Are the conflicts good or bad? What are the major areas where inter-departmental conflicts take place? The most important thing is that how these conflicts could be minimized? Whose responsibility it is to do this?

Benchmarking - A case on Tap changers

Tap changers

A tap changer is a device fitted to power transformers for regulation of the output voltage to required levels. This is normally achieved by changing the ratios of the transformers on the system by altering the number of turns in one winding of the appropriate transformer/s. Supply authorities are under obligation to their customers to maintain the supply voltage between certain limits. Tap changers offer variable control to keep the supply voltage within these limits. About 96% of all power transformers today above 10 MVA incorporate on load tap changers as a means of voltage regulation.

Tap changers can be on load or off load. On load tap changers generally consist of a diverter switch and a selector switch operating as a unit to effect transfer current from one voltage tap to the next. On load tap changers were introduced to power transformers as a means of on load voltage control more than 60 years ago.

Types of Tap Changers

There are two major designs of tap changers in use

in the industry. They are,

Flange mounted tap changers – They are preferred for ratings up to 25 MVA and 66 KV Voltage class. Mainly used in South African, USA and Indian continent.

In tank on load tap changers generally used for medium and higher rating of the Transformers all over the world.

Comparison

The In Tank tap changers offer following advantages:

- Less maintenance frequency.

- Compact for high voltage and high current ratings

- High contact life.

RTC Tap changers

RTC started manufacturing Flange Mounted tap changers in 1966 as per the design of English Electric (UK). The In tank tap changers were introduced in the year 1998. Year ended, March 31, 2012, the tap changers contribute 55% share to the total revenue of RTC. Of this, close to Rs.70 crores come from flange mounted tap changers and about Rs.15 crores come from in tank tap changers. In the former, RTC is a leader in India with a market share close to 70%.

In order to maintain their leadership, RTC is exploring new technologies in tap changers. This includes vacuum tap changers also.

Global players

The major players in the world are,

Asea Brown Boveri (ABB) from Switzerland a major global player for flange mounted tap changers and Intank Tap changers and also hold IPR on some products.

MachinenfabricReinhausen (MR) from Germany has more than 70 years of experience with on load tap changers. They have an estimated annual turnover of Rs.2000 crores and enjoy a global market share of 75%. They are the leaders in In tank tap changers in the world and also hold IPR on the product. Competition from Huaming/China and Hyundai/South Korea is also emerging.

Markets for Tap changers

The Indian market for tap changers has virtually saturated with an annual growth rate of less than 10%. As such, if RTC has to grow, they will have to seriously plan a strategy to enter global markets. They will have to withstand the competition mainly from ABB and MR. In order to outsmart them, RTC will have to develop products which are at par if not superior to these manufacturers. They can further take advantage of low cost manufacturing to maintain their share in Indian markets and to penetrate the global markets.

To achieve the objectives, RTC will have to benchmark these two companies in major aspects.

Let us understand the principles of Benchmarking.

Benchmarking is the process of comparing one's business processes and performance metrics to industry bests or best practices from other industries. Dimensions typically measured are quality, time and cost. In the process of benchmarking, management identifies the best firms in their industry, or in another industry where similar processes exist, and compare the results and processes of those studied (the "targets") to one's own results and processes. In this way, they learn how well the targets perform and, more importantly, the business processes that explain why these firms are successful.

Benchmarking is used to measure performance using a specific indicator (cost per unit of measure, productivity per unit of measure, cycle time of x per unit of measure or defects per unit of measure) resulting in a metric of performance that is then compared to others.

Also referred to as "best practice benchmarking" or "process benchmarking", this process is used in management and particularly strategic management, in which organizations evaluate various aspects of their processes in relation to best practice companies' processes, usually within a peer group defined for the purposes of comparison. This then allows organizations to develop plans on how to make improvements or adapt specific best practices, usually with the aim of increasing some aspect of performance. Benchmarking may be a one-off event, but is often treated as a continuous process in which organizations continually seek to improve their practices.

Benefits and use

In 2008, a comprehensive survey on benchmarking was commissioned by The Global Benchmarking Network, a network of benchmarking centers representing 22 countries. Over 450 organizations responded from over 40 countries. The results showed that:

- Mission and Vision Statements and Customer (Client) Surveys are the most used (by 77%) of organizations, followed by SWOT analysis (72%), and Informal (No specific performance standards) Benchmarking (68%), Performance Benchmarking was used by 49% and Best Practice Benchmarking (39%).

- The tools that are likely to increase in popularity the most over the next three years are Performance Benchmarking, SWOT, and Best Practice Benchmarking. Over 60% of organizations that are not currently using these tools indicated they are likely to use them in the next three years.

Procedure

There is no single benchmarking process that has been universally adopted. The wide appeal and acceptance of benchmarking has led to the emergence of benchmarking methodologies. One seminal book is Boxwell's Benchmarking for Competitive Advantage (1994). The first book on benchmarking, written and published by Kaiser Associates, is a practical guide. Robert Camp (1989) developed a 12-stage approach to benchmarking.

The 12 stage methodology consists of:

- Select subject
- Define the process
- Identify potential partners
- Identify data sources
- Collect data and select partners
- Determine the gap
- Establish process differences
- Target future performance
- Communicate
- Adjust goal
- Implement
- Review and recalibrate

The following is an example of a typical benchmarking methodology:

Identify problem areas: Because benchmarking can be applied to any business process or function, a range of research techniques may be required. They include informal conversations with customers, employees, or suppliers; exploratory research techniques such as focus groups; or in-depth marketing research, quantitative research, surveys, questionnaires, re-engineering analysis, process mapping, quality control variance reports, financial ratio analysis, or simply reviewing cycle times or other performance indicators.

Identify organizations that are leaders in these areas:

Look for the very best in any industry and in any country. Consult customers, suppliers, financial analysts, trade associations, and magazines to determine which companies are worthy of study.

Survey companies for measures and practices: Companies target specific business processes using detailed surveys of measures and practices to identify business process alternatives of leading companies. Surveys are typically masked to protect confidential data by neutral associations and consultants.

Visit the "best practice" companies to identify leading edge practices: Companies typically agree to mutually exchange information beneficial to all parties in a benchmarking group and share the results within the group.

Implement new and improved business practices: Take the leading edge practices and develop implementation plans which include identification of specific opportunities, funding the project and selling the ideas to the organization for the purpose of gaining demonstrated value from the process.

Costs.

The three main types of costs in benchmarking are:

Visit Costs - This includes hotel rooms, travel costs, meals, a token gift, and lost labor time.

Time Costs - Members of the benchmarking team will be investing time in researching problems, finding exceptional companies to study, visits, and implementation. This will take them away from their regular tasks for part of each day so additional staff might be required.

Benchmarking Database Costs - Organizations that institutionalize benchmarking into their daily procedures find it is useful to create and maintain a database of best practices and the companies associated with each best practice now.

The cost of benchmarking can substantially be reduced through utilizing the many internet resources that have sprung up over the last few years. These aim to capture benchmarks and best practices from organizations, business sectors and countries to make the benchmarking process much quicker and cheaper.

Technical/product benchmarking

The technique initially used to compare existing corporate strategies with a view to achieving the best possible performance in new situations, has recently been extended to the comparison of technical products. This process is usually referred to as "technical benchmarking" or "product benchmarking". Its use is well-developed within the automotive industry ("automotive benchmarking"), where it is vital to design products that match precise user expectations, at minimal cost, by applying the best technologies available worldwide. Data is obtained by fully disassembling existing cars and their systems. Such analyses were initially carried out in-house by car makers and their suppliers. However, as these analyses are expensive, they are increasingly being outsourced to companies who specialize in this area. Outsourcing has enabled a drastic decrease in costs for each company (by cost sharing) and the development of efficient tools (standards, software).

Types

Process benchmarking - the initiating firm focuses its observation and investigation of business processes with a goal of identifying and observing the best practices from one or more benchmark firms. Activity analysis will be required where the objective is to benchmark cost and efficiency; increasingly applied to back-office processes where outsourcing may be a consideration.

Financial benchmarking - performing a financial analysis and comparing the results in an effort to assess your overall competitiveness and productivity.

Benchmarking from an investor perspective- extending the benchmarking universe to also compare to peer companies that can be considered alternative investment opportunities from the perspective of an investor.

Performance benchmarking - allows the initiator firm to assess their competitive position by comparing products and services with those of target firms.

Product benchmarking - the process of designing new products or upgrades to current ones. This process can sometimes involve reverse engineering which is taking apart competitors products to find strengths and weaknesses.

Strategic benchmarking - involves observing how others compete. This type is usually not industry specific, meaning it is best to look at other industries.

Functional benchmarking - a company will focus its benchmarking on a single function to improve the operation of that particular function. Complex functions such as Human Resources, Finance and Accounting and Information and Communication Technology are unlikely to be directly comparable in cost and efficiency terms and may need to be disaggregated into processes to make valid comparison.

Best-in-class benchmarking - involves studying the leading competitor or the company that best carries out a specific function.

Operational benchmarking - embraces everything from staffing and productivity to office flow and analysis of procedures performed.[5]

Tools

Benchmarking software can be used to organize large and complex amounts of information. Software packages can extend the concept of benchmarking and competitive analysis by allowing individuals to handle such large and complex amounts or strategies. Such tools support different types of benchmarking (see above) and can reduce the above costs significantly.

Strategy for RTC

It is interesting to note that MR has entered in joint venture (JV) in different countries. They have a JV in India under the name of Easun-MR based in Chennai. Initially, they offered in tank tap changers at 20% higher prices than of RTC. However, now they are matching

RTC prices to penetrate the Indian markets. Not only MR has a superior product, they also have the best testing laboratory in the country. MR had collaboration in China which expired in 1995.

Not only for tap changers, but for all present and future products, RTC will have to give due importance to the strategies to be adopted on Benchmarking. At the same time, they will have to ensure that they do not infringe IPR Act which can land them in legal wrangle which may result in lost opportunities, delays and litigation costs.

The questions for which RTC will have to seek answers are,

- How RTC should put to use the concept of benchmarking as a competitive strategy?
- Benchmarking decisions will have to be taken with respect to,
- Which leader?
- What Product range?
- Designing or reverse engineering?
- If reverse engineering, how to not infringe IPR?
- Quality and reliability?
- Any others

Developing Marketing Strategy for Mobile Elevated Work Platforms (MEWP)

This product line falls under the field of Material Handling Equipments in which Sigma Engineers entered only in 2008 as a part of growth strategy. Sigma is a manufacturer of Electrical Motors in the range of 5 HP to 200 HP. As such, it was a diversification for Sigma from electrical equipments line.

Sigma entered in a joint venture (JV) with a Chinese company named Sinoboom (Sino). The arrangement between the two companies covers the following aspects:

o   Sigma uses the basic design of Sinoboom. Modifications are suggested as per the requirements of Indian clients.

o   The mobile equipments are received in completely knocked down (CKD) form by Sigma. from China.

o   Customization is done by Sigma as per the requirements of customers through outsourcing.

o   Sigma has made many modifications such as revolving light with buzzers, electrical changes and few others.

o   Mobile equipments up to 20 meters' are

supplied under Sigma name and are quoted in Indian Rupees.

o The equipments above 20 meters' go on the name of Sinoboom and are quoted in US Dollars.

Mobile Elevated Work Platforms

Basically, these are different types of lifts that are used for variety of applications. As they are mobile (either manually driven or self-propelled by DC Power or Diesel Engine), they are named as mobile equipments.

The present product mix of mobile equipments is as follows:

o Electrical powered scissor lifts (DC/AC)

o Electrical powered articulated boom lifts (DC/AC)

o Engine powered articulated boom lifts (Only by diesel engine)

o Engine powered telescopic boom lifts (Only by diesel engine)

All are operated hydraulically.

Target customers

Presently, Sigma caters to following market segments:

o Manufacturing industries

o Multiplexes and shopping malls

o Pre-engineered buildings

o Large Private Hospitals

o   Star category hotels

It is interesting to note that there are many other segments which hold potential which are not yet tapped by Sigma. One of them includes fire fighting operations particularly in high rise buildings in metro towns. It is interesting to note that Pune Municipal Corporation (PMC) some time back imported a Truck Mounted Telescopic Rescue Ladder from a European country which can go up to 70 meters. It cost them around Rs.13 crores. There have been media reports that it is not functional and there are problems of maintenance.

Market size

The market for such MEWPs has opened in India only since last 5-6 years. No systematic research has been done to estimate the market size in India. On the basis of tenders floated across the country, it has been estimated that around 200-300 numbers of different types of mobile equipments are bought in the country. In Rupee terms, this will amount to around Rs.70-80 crores per annum. Presently, the Indian market is growing at 25-30% per annum.

The export potential also looks bright particularly in neighboring countries and developing countries in African Region.

Competition

The competition for mobile equipments in Indian markets is limited. In organized sector, there is only Vanjax based in Chennai with maximum lift height of 20 Metres. There are few in unorganized sectors who are mainly traders importing it from different countries. They include JLG from USA who has opened a marketing office in Delhi. The others are Genic (USA) and Hanlotte (France) besides Sigma who represents Sinoboom.

Market share

JLG is the market leader in all types of mobile equipments. Sigma has a market share of around 10% and they are leaders in Scissor Type Equipments. There are close to 600 potential customers across the country of which Sigma has close to 90 customers.

Product Line Contribution

Sigma achieved a turnover of around Rs.5.5 crores in 2011-12. The estimated forecast for 2012-13 is Rs.7.5 crores. This sale mainly comprises of regular shop floor material handling equipments and partially of scissor type MEWPs.

Type	% Contribution	Margin %
Telescopic (Above 22 meters)	10	40
Articulated (Up to 22 meters)	12	30
Scissor type (Max.16meters)	25	20
Aluminum multi mast	15	15

Marketing strategy of Sigma

As was mentioned earlier, Sigma started marketing mobile equipments since 2008. As a policy, it was decided to first concentrate in Maharashtra to begin with. In the third year, neighboring states were added. As against this, Vanjax has now reached all over India.

Sigma has exported two scissor type equipments to Nigeria and Bangladesh. However, there have been no systematic and sustained efforts in export marketing. There is no restriction on the same from the Chinese partner.

Marketing Mix

The marketing mix can be identified for mobile equipments as follows:

Product mix: There are close to 20 different models available in different versions as given above.

Price mix: Markup pricing is used.

Distribution mix: Presently, Sigma has appointed dealers in Chennai, Nasik, Aurangabad and Hardwar. What is the logic behind this is not known?

Promotion mix: Sigma participates in exhibitions across the country held on material handling equipment's. Most of the enquiries are generated through the same. Enquiries are also generated through dealers and personal visits.

Manpower: Presently, there are 18 persons including operators who are working in this division. This manpower is inadequate for installing mobile equipments over 20 meters.

With the above background, Sigma will have to give a serious thought on many aspects of strategic management. These will include the following:

- o Sigma's core competency being in electrical equipment and allied industry, should they be in this diversified field of material handling? How much Sigma should commit in this sector to make it a profitable and growth line?

- o Should Sigma continue to import these products or think of setting a manufacturing unit of their own? With what kind of investments, payback period and ROI?

- o What should be the strategic plan for next five years? Which segments they should target?

- o What should be the organization structure for next five years projections?

- o What strategies they should put to use in distribution and promotion?

- o Should Sigma think of developing an export strategy?

Your suggestions on the above and any other aspects are solicited.

Developing a Positioning Strategy for Aluminum Electrolytic Capacitors (AEC)

RTC started its manufacturing operations at Aurangabad in the year 1972 when it started manufacturing variety of plastic film capacitors. Today, RTC is a leader in professional grade capacitors in India manufacturing more than 10,000 types of capacitors. A partial list of types of capacitors manufactured by RTC is given below:

Range of Capacitors

Capacitors, passive

Capacitors, fixed, paper

Capacitors, fixed, polycarbonate

Capacitors, fixed, polyester

Capacitors, fixed, polyethylene terephthalate (PET) polyester film

Capacitors, fixed, polypropylene (PP)

Capacitors, fixed, polystyrene

Capacitors, fixed, poly tetrafluoro ethylene (PTFE)

Capacitors, fixed, high voltage (HV)

Capacitors, fixed, low voltage (LV)

Capacitors, fixed, miniature and subminiature

Capacitors, fixed, power factor correction

Capacitors, fixed, ignition

Capacitors, fixed, pulse/impulse generator

Capacitors, fixed, induction furnace

Capacitors, plastic dielectric

RTC was always chalking out growth strategies in product extension. The above capacitors mostly find applications in entertainment equipments like TV, Tape recorders, telecommunications and many others.

In the year 2010 it was decided to extend the range and take up the manufacture of Aluminum Electrolytic Capacitors (AEC). It was decided that to begin with, RTC will start trading in AEC. As such, trading activities were started only in January 2012. The first billing was done in April 2012. As per the present plans, full fledged manufacturing will start in Aurangabad from July 2013. A capital investment of close to Rs.246 lakhs will be made till 2017.

Electrolytic capacitors

Professional grade AEC's are recommended for use in ripple current filtering on account of compact size, low ESR and high ripple current handling capacities. Please see the attached product brochure. They are more suitable for low voltage applications at lower frequencies.

The three main parts in AEC are,

o Forming voltage

o Paper

o Electrolyte.

Together, they make an assembly, radials, PCB mounting and screw terminals. The last one is of high value.

Target customers

Presently, the AEC's are marketed to UPS manufacturers and welding manufacturers. There are potential applications in telecom and other sectors. For the former, the major customers include, Uniline, Emerson, DB Power, Numeric and others. There are close to 150 potential customers for AEC in India of which CTR has been able to reach around 50 customers so far.

Market size

As per secondary data available, the world market for AEC has been estimated at around USD 21 Billion (Approximately Rs. 1,90,000 crores). The Indian market for the size in which CTR will be operating has been estimated at Rs. 65-70 crores per annum growing at 10-15% per annum.

Major competitors

Nippon Chemicon (NCC) is considered as world leader. There are South Korean and Chinese manufacturers who are mostly in volume business in telecom sector.

Following players are active in Indian markets:

Imported players

- o Kendil (Italy) who have a JV under the name of IKEM based at Bangalore.

- o Itelcnd (Italy)

- o Ducate (USA)

- o Jinghai (China)

Domestic players

Alcon (Nasik): They are the market leaders with annual turnover of the order of Rs. 28 crores for AEC. They have around 70% market share. Sarda (Bangalore) with annual turnover of the order of Rs. 8 crore. Rescon (Pune) with annual turnover of the order of Rs. 3 crores.

Marketing mix of RTC

Product mix: The attached product literature gives the range of AEC.

Price mix: RTC is offering a better quality than Alcon but at a lower price

Distribution mix: Presently, RTC goes for direct marketing and also has 11 Dealers across the country.

Promotion mix: Personal selling is resorted with OEM's. Presently there is only one person looking after marketing

Future plans

The target for AEC for the year 2012-13 is Rs. 1 crore. The present delivery period is around 8 weeks which shows the nature of seller's market. RTC has set a target of Rs. 10 crores after 5 years. They plan to enter export markets from 2016 onwards. It is interesting to note that after the grid collapse in the north some six months back, the sale of UPS shot up by more than 20% thereby increasing the demand for AECs.

As RTC has been rather late in the market, they will have to think of chalking a successful marketing strategy. However, it is felt that the more important aspect will be developing a positioning strategy.

What exactly is meant by Product Positioning Strategy? Read the note given below:

Product Positioning Strategy

In marketing, **positioning** is the process by which marketers try to create an image or identity in the minds of their target market for its product, brand, or organization.

Re-positioning involves changing the identity of a product, relative to the identity of competing products.

De-positioning involves attempting to change the identity of competing products, relative to the identity of your own product.

Positioning is a concept in marketing which was first introduced by Jack Trout ("Industrial Marketing"

109

Magazine- June/1969) and then popularized by Al Ries and Jack Trout in their bestseller book "Positioning - The Battle for Your Mind." (McGraw-Hill 1981)

What most will agree on is that Positioning is something (perception) that happens in the minds of the target market. It is the aggregate perception the market has of a particular company, product or service in relation to their perceptions of the competitors in the same category. It will happen whether or not a company's management is proactive, reactive or passive about the on-going process of evolving a position. But a company can positively influence the perceptions through enlightened strategic actions.

Positioning Statement As written in the highly revered book Crossing the Chasm (Copyright 1991, by Geoffrey Moore, HarperCollins Publishers), the position statement is a phrase so formulated: For (target customer) who (statement of the need or opportunity), the (product name) is a (product category) that (statement of key benefit – that is, compelling reason to buy). Unlike (primary competitive alternative), our product (statement of primary differentiation).

Differentiation in the context of business is what a company can hang its hat on that no other business can. For example, for some companies this is being the least expensive. Other companies credit themselves with being the first or the fastest. Whatever it is a business can use to stand out from the rest is called differentiation. Differentiation in today's over-crowded marketplace is a business imperative, not only in terms of a company's success, but also for its continuing survival.

Product positioning process

Generally, the product positioning process involves:

Defining the market in which the product or brand will compete (who the relevant buyers are) and identifying the attributes (also called dimensions) they desire.

Collecting information from a sample of customers about their perceptions of each product on the relevant attributes

- Determine each product's share of mind

- Determine each product's current location in the product space

- Determine the target market's preferred combination of attributes.

- Examine the fit between.

Alternative strategies for product positioning

Philip Kotler (Marketing Management –Analysis, Planning & Control – 12 Edition) has recommended six alternative positioning strategies:

- Positioning with respect to product features, specifications

- Positioning with respect to benefits assured

- Position with respect to user category, target customers

- Positioning with respect to usage occasion

- Positioning with respect to competitors

- Repositioning or change of image

Key result areas

RTC will have to identify key result areas. Some of them will include,

- Early acceptance of its AEC in the market

- Developing competitive strategies, particularly the negative marketing that may be adopted by market leader Alcon.

- Consistency in availability and quality of major raw materials needed to manufacture AEC.

- Developing the right marketing organization

Give your recommendations on all and any other aspects for AEC.

Marketing Strategy for Power Factor Correction Capacitors (PFCC)

It is a fact that world over the energy costs are rising. This is because of demand increasing faster than the supply. All countries are looking for alternative sources of energy besides the traditional sources of energy which included hydel, thermal and nuclear powers. In last 20 years or more, non-conventional forms of energy have been developed. They include wind energy, gas based energy generation, solar power, cogeneration of power from agriculture waste, ceramic fuels and many others.

All electrical loads which operate by means of magnetic fields such as electrical motors, transformers, fluorescent lighting and others consume two types of energy namely Active Power and Reactive Power. The former is used by the loads to meet it's functional requirements whereas the latter is used to meet it's magnetic field requirements as also magnetic losses.

Reactive power results in increased costs. It is necessary to reduce the reactive power to optimize system performance. Capacitors are most cost effective and reliable static device which can supply reactive power and maintain power factor close to unity.

LT Power Capacitors are used for improving the power factor for use under dynamic loads and wide voltage fluctuation conditions in single and three phase applications, ensuring reduction in harmonic distortion. The typical payback period for investing in PFCC is less than a year.

RTC's entry in PFCC

RTC sensed an opportunity for PFCC in India. No systematic market research was carried out. However, as leaders in manufacturing professional grade plastic film capacitors, they felt that they can make a foray in this line also. It must be noted that PFCC is totally a different product in design and applications as compared to passive capacitors.

RTC started with PFCC as trading item buying from a Nasik based company. The full fledged manufacturing commenced only in December 2011. They have an installed capacity of 3000 kvr per day. The capital investment on this project by 2017 will be of the order of Rs. 3.5 crores.

Manufacturing of PFCC is labor intensive. Presently, RTC has 30 persons in the manufacture and they depend considerably on sub-contractors.

Target customers

It has been estimated that the market for PFCC is of the order of Rs. 500 crore per annum growing at around 20% per annum. The potential is half for LT & HT PFCC each. RTC presently has plans only to be in LT PFCC. For manufacturing HT PFCC, a different set up of capabilities, manufacturing and testing facilities is required.

The target customers for LT PFCC are as follows:

- Industry (Actual users)

- Electrical panel manufacturers (OEM's)

- State Electricity Boards (SEB's)

- Electrical contractors'

- Project consultants

SEB's encourage user industries to install PFCCs.

Major competitors

PFCC is comparatively a simple engineering product requiring moderate investments. The technology, machinery and raw materials are easily available. As such, there are close to 36 manufacturers of which almost 20 manufacturers are recognized by IEEMA. SEB's require BIS specifications.

The major players in this line are as follows:

- Epcos, L & T
- Schinder
- Matrix
- Neptune
- Shreem capacitors
- Subodhan

- Prabodhan

- Standard

Barring few, most of the manufacturers are in unorganized sector lacking marketing strengths.

Marketing Planning & Strategy Formulation

Planning: Planning is ideally a search in the future to situate the organization in the present to take care of threats and opportunities. It sets up specific objectives for a defined time period. Planning does two things viz setting of objectives translated into vision, mission, goals, targets and quotas and designing strategies to achieve the objectives.

Strategy: Strategy are decision variables to achieve the objectives. They could be long term as well as short term. Strategic marketing is defined under STP.

Segmenting: Identify market segments with distinctly different characteristics. For industrial (B2B) marketing, they mainly include geographical and end use segments.

Targeting: Identify the segments which offer the best potential at a particular time. The organization then focuses on the same with its resources.

Positioning: Positioning is basically a communication strategy. The marketing communication for B2B normally includes personal selling, sales promotion, public relations and occasionally advertising in technical media.

Al Ries & Jack Trout in the early seventies came out with positioning strategy. It has nothing to do with the product but deals with the minds of the customers. It aims at creating a certain image in the minds of the customers vis-à-vis competitors.

Positioning of PFCC of RTC

RTC also manufactures Electrical Capacitors (EC). The annual turnover is of the order of Rs. 2 crores per annum. The major application of EC is to give running torque to electrical motors.

RTC will have to think on the following issues:

o With so much competition for PFCC in the Indian markets, what marketing strategy be developed?

o How STP should be put to use?

o With Electrical Capacitors in the range of RTC, how the PFCC should be positioned to avoid any type of confusion in the minds of the target customers?

The present dealer/stockiest network may not be useful since market segment and customer base is totally different as compared to present range of electronics capacitor. Recommend the Channels of Distribution that should be used for marketing PFCC?

Any other aspects that need to be considered in areas of manufacturing, supply chain management, outsourcing and any others? Offer your suggestions.

Arklite Speciality Lamps Ltd. (UV Air Purifier)

"Indians are a funny people. When it will come to personal hygiene, they are best in the world. However, when it comes to public hygiene, they are found wanting". These were the opening comments made by Dr. Avinash Kulkarni Chairman of Arklite Speciality Lamps Ltd. 'This is contrary to the Westerners. Indians will take bath three times in a day; will wash their mouth after every meal. However, when they are in public, spitting is very common. Perhaps, after Chinese, Indians are the biggest spitters in the world. They will throw garbage anywhere, urinate and defecate on the roads. In comparison, Europeans may take bath once in two-three days, will seldom wash their mouths after taking food. However, when it will come to public hygiene, they maintain strict discipline. You will never see the sights in Europe which we commonly see in India.'

Avinash was addressing a press conference on the launch of his new product, namely, Ultraviolet Air Purification System. There were close to thirty journalists from different newspapers and TV media.

'This is the product of our indigenous R & D which will be suitable in all public places where you would like to have clean and pure air. Our system will destroy bad odour and will kill germs and bacteria which cause the same. Commercially, this can also be called as Stench Remover.

Avinash is the first generation entrepreneur who always prided on his innovative abilities.

Entrepreneurship

Avinash hails from Indore where he had his schooling. He had a brilliant academic career. He joined Indian Institute of Technology (IIT), Powai and obtained his BTech in the year 1963. He worked for a couple of years in India and went to USA for higher studies. He obtained PhD in Metallurgy & Material Science from University of Pennsylvania, an Ivy League University. He joined Westinghouse Electric Corp, a well known manufacturer of electrical equipments. During his 8 year stint there, besides obtaining an MBA through an evening school he also received a Citation as an Inventor from Westinghouse for securing five US Patents. It was during his Westinghouse stint, the Entrepreneurial Bug bit him and he decided to return to India and be on his own.

'What type of business one should start' is always the question which probes minds of all would be entrepreneurs. Avinash toyed with few ideas and finally decided to take up the manufacture of halogen lamps. Mahendra Shah, his fellow employee at Westinghouse, decided to join him in this venture. It was decided that the project will be set up in Pune. While he was still working in USA, he started the feasibility study for his proposed venture with the help of development agencies in Maharashtra. The learning experience on all facets of starting a business was unique with some good memories and some bad. He found out to his dismay that the License & Inspector Raj had not only survived since independence but was thriving. The entrepreneurs have to run from pillar to post to get all the clearances that are needed to start a business in India. This included obtaining industrial shed, power, water, finance, raw materials and many other inputs. It may get frustrating but one has to doggedly pursue them. There are shortcuts available in the form of bribing the right authorities to obtain clearances even for straight and simple formalities. Ethical as he is, he decided that even if it takes time, he will not give bribes to obtain any clearances. It took 11 months to get possession of his industrial shed and another 10 months to make the first lamp.

The Project

As it happens in all success stories in USA, Avinash started his company on a modest scale under the name of Litex Electricals Private Limited (Litex). The halogen lamps have a better lighting than the ordinary bulbs. With machines, mostly fabricated by the two partners, Litex started manufacturing in a small way and it took 5 years to reach 100 lamps per day! Another 5 years to reach 1000 lamps a day, with current production being 5000 lamps a day. Avinash was mostly a technical person and hence how to market these lamps was a big question in front of him. Luckily, this problem was resolved when all the major names in Indian markets like Mysore Lamps, Sylvania Laxman, Bajaj, ECE, Crompton, Kalpana Lamps, and others agreed to buy them and market them under their brand names. A lamp was directly marketed to these big names at a price of Rs.80/ only. The OEM's marked it up and were offering it to end users at Rs.180/-.

The OEM's started demanding more and Litex was too happy to oblige. They developed machinery and the volumes went up from less than 100 a day to present volume of 5000 lamps per day. During this time, they also developed more variety of lamps for applications like Photocopier Lamps, Infra Red (IR) Lamps and later Laser Pumping Lamps. From just 10 persons to begin with, the company has now over 100 persons working with them.

Diversification

Encouraged, Avinash and Mahendra started up a second company under the name of Litel Infrared Systems Pvt. Ltd which manufactures process heating systems using Litex made IR lamps. Mahendra is the MD of this unit promoted in 1987. Pramod Shringarpure, who was a Vice President at Kirloskar Consultants Ltd. joined the company as a founder Director and was a key person in the venture.

Both Litex and Litel have always been profitable, dividend paying companies since their inception.

Accolades

The efforts of Litex were well received and rewarded. Following awards were received by the company as well as by Avinash.

o   G. S. Parkhe Industrial Merit Award by MCCIA in 1982 andin 1985.

o   First Prize of National Award as an outstanding SSI Entrepreneur from President of India(1985).

o   National Award for Excellence in R&D in Electrical and Electronic sector from DSIR, Government of India (1991.

Avinash also got active with local Mahrattha Chamber of Commerce & Industries (MCCIA) and was elected as Chairman of the Small Scale wing. He also got actively involved with Electric Lighting and Component Manufacturers Association (ELCOMA), an apex body of Rs. 6000 crore lighting industry and became its all India President for two terms (2002-4). Currently all India President of Indian Society of Lighting Engineers (ISLE) for a four year term (2007-11).

Encouraged by his performance, his younger brother Dr. Ravindra Kulkarni, a PhD in Engineering from Columbia University, New York and based in USA for 20 years also decided to return to India in 1990 to set up his own Chemical business. He started manufacturing Silicon Oil which found wide applications in different types of industries, including mould release in foundry industry, textiles and in the manufacture of condoms to name a few.

Birth of Arklite

In the year 1996 it was decided to set up a closely held limited company under the name of Arklite Speciality Lamps Ltd. at Chakan, some 30 kms away from Pune in a notified backward area to obtain backward area benefits. Avinash accepted the responsibility as the Chairman & CTO of the company and Ravi became the Managing Director.

Present activities

The present status of Arklite is given below:

*   Sales turnover of Rs. 11 crores year ended March 31, 2009.

*   Product range includes:

    # Metal Halide Lamps

    # Ultra Violet Lamps

    # Graphic Art and High Wattage MH Lamps (MBIL)

    # UV Systems for Air Disinfection

*   Has two manufacturing units: Export Oriented Unit (EOU) to cater to major customers in Europe and USA and a Domestic Tariff Unit (DTU) to serve OE lamp customers in India and to manufacture and market UV systems.

*   Employs 200 persons including 25 technical persons, including 3 in sales and marketing.

*   Lamp marketing to OE customers in India and abroad; export account for 60% of sales. Country wide distribution network is being set up for the UV systems marketing.

*   Appointed a full time Director, 100% dedicated to run company's operation in Chakan in June 2008.

Development of Air Purifier for Stench Elimination

The basic philosophy in developing this product included the following facts for the Indian markets:

o   Inadequate use of water

o   Poor usage practices

o   Poor maintenance

o   Poor plumbing methods

o   Ubiquitous, Unbearable, Unpleasant Smell in & outside the toilet areas

o   Unhygienic environment

o   Growth of Bacteria, Mold & Fungi

o   Chemicals or repellents to suppress the stench

o   Masking Methods

o   Temporary solution with low product life

o   High Operational Cost

Advantages

o   Stench Elimination by odour destruction

o   Prevents Molds & Fungi formation

o   Kills bacteria

o   No usage of chemicals

o   Clean, Effective & Environment friendly

o   Low running cost

o   Easy installation

The system comprises of Arklite make 'Ultraviolet Lamp' which generates UV radiation and Ozone. Ozone oxidizes all volatile organic compounds which cause stench. UV radiation kills micro-organisms such as bacteria, viruses, molds, algae and protozoa.

Product range

The company developed five different models to choose from

o   S-01 - 6W Ozone forming without fan

o   S-02 - 11W Non Ozone Forming with fan

o   S-03 - 11W Ozone Forming with fan

o   L-01 - 21W Ozone forming with fan

o   L-02 - 21W Non Ozone forming with fan

The prices range between Rs.4000/ to Rs.7000/ per unit, inclusive of all duties & taxes.

The initial orders included public urinals of Pune Municipal Corporation, hospitals and toilets in factories where Avinash had contacts. However, an overall marketing strategy was yet to be developed.

Market Research

A local market research agency was engaged who gave an encouraging report on the potential for this system. The brief findings are given below:

During the market research, contacts were made with hotels, restaurants, hostels, educational institutes, corporate offices and others. The sample size was 50. The coverage was in upcoming areas of Aundh, Baner and Hinjewadi in Pune city only.

o 72% of respondents reported that they have the problem of stench in their toilets.

o The present methods used to eliminate stench in that order includes washing by phenyl (80%), installing exhaust fans (70%), keeping air fresheners in the toilet (68%) and using aerosol cans (2%).

o Almost 82% respondents are aware of the harmful effects of using the above alternatives for removing stench from the toilets. They would welcome a safer and superior product for this purpose.

o 82% respondents have no knowledge of UV Air Purifiers.

o Close to 50% of the respondents showed a desire to get a demonstration of the product.

o 30% respondents showed their willingness to buy the product, 12% respondents said that they will decide only after seeing a demonstration. 36% respondents felt that the price was high and they will not be immediately interested in buying the product.

22% did not offer any opinion on buying. It is very much possible to transform these 'Disinterested Parties' in taking a buying decision.

Overall, the product has a good potential provided the prices are kept reasonable. The target market will comprise of institutional buyers like restaurants, corporate offices and educational institutes.

It is felt that a dual distribution strategy of Direct Marketing for bulk orders and through a Dealer Network for retail orders will be more effective.

An effective communication strategy will be necessary to create awareness and to generate the leads.

Close to six months have passed since the product has been ready. The sales have been marginal, no where coming closer to the forecasts made by the Market Research Consultants. Avinash is wondering whether something is wrong with product or is it because of lack of planning, strategy and marketing efforts.

What you have to do is to seek the answers to following questions:

- How to estimate all India potential for the product?

- What share of the market they should aim at?

- What marketing decision variables under 4 P's they must develop?

- Who are their likely competitors?

- How should they position the product?

- How much marketing budget they must provide for a year?

- How should they do allocation of this budget over different marketing sub-functions?

- What further innovations they should come out with this product?

- Should they explore overseas markets? How?

Manman Surgical Manufacturing Company (MSMC)

He did not go to the prestigious IIT's or IIM's in the country to study. He even did not go to any reputed engineering college. However, today, he is involved in designing, developing and manufacturing some very sophisticated surgical power tools in the country.

Meet **Mr. Madhukar Gokhale**, popularly known as 'Manman' Gokhale across the country.

Personal History

Madhukar was born on October 22, 1940 in a typical middle class Maharashtrian family with three brothers. His father ran a coal depot. He studied at Pune's Fergusson College till Inter Science. He did his Diploma in Draughtsmanship from Cusrow Wadia Technical Institute, Pune and went to S. V. Government Polytechnic, Bhopal from where he got Diploma in Mechanical Engineering (1967). He worked with Bharat Heavy Electricals Ltd, Bhopal for 2 years on the shop floor. He returned to Pune and worked for 16 years with Tata Motors Ltd. as a Training Officer (1967-83). Since 1978 he started developing surgical tools & accessories.

If you look at his education and practical experience, one feels amazed how and why he took up to manufacturing Surgical Power Tools (SPT)?

His younger brother Manohar Gokhale became a Neuro Surgeon. Unfortunately, he did not live long. Madhukar used to accompany his brother during the operations. His brother and other surgeons used to

talk about non-availability of the tools at affordable prices, improvements needed and so on. This prompted Madhukar to start experimenting. He has in-born mechanical aptitude which helped in coming with indigenous technologies in SPT's. In order to honor the memory of his late brother, he came up with the name **Manman.**

The hobbies of Madhukar include portrait sketching, painting and Photography. When he was young, he also gave shows in magic.

Vision & Mission

Even though he never came out with a clear definition, Madhukar was very clear what he would like to do. This included a strong feeling of 'Swadeshi' and creating **Manman**- a Made in India brand to reckon.

He also felt that his products should be of best quality and at the same time affordable to all.

Present status

Presently, there are 5 companies under Manman Group of companies employing close to 70 persons with a combined turnover of around Rs.7 crores. Except for MSMC, all others are either proprietorships or partnerships in the family itself. The family comprises of Madhukar, his brother, his daughter (who is the CEO) and other close relatives. A tragedy happened some 12 years back when the young and dynamic son of Madhukar died in an accident at a young age of 30. This completely shattered Madhukar but he somehow forgot his grief and put himself full time in the business. His daughter-in-law also assists him in the business. He has two grandsons aged 17 & 12 respectively and studying. The group has two manufacturing facilities, a central administrative office and an electronics laboratory.

The group does not have any highly qualified staff. Most of the members are either relatives or are recommended by others. Most were raw persons who were shaped by Madhukar in being useful. As such, the group can be called a family concern. A formal organization structure is missing and everybody does all types of jobs.

The company is making profit year after year. The present PAT is at around 8% of the total turnover.

Product Mix

Today, the company makes more than 20 different types of Surgical Power Tools. This includes Universal Bone Drill, Sagittal Saw Hand pieces, Flexible Reamers, Reverse Forward Hand pieces, Reciprocating Saw Hand pieces, Bone Cutting, and Drilling & Reaming Systems. The entire range can be seen on their website www. manmanindia.com. The prices range from Rs.10,000 to Rs.300,000/ depending on the sophistication needed.

Unlike other products, his export prices are higher by almost 50% than the domestic prices!

The company has been winning year after year prestigious Parkhe Awards for original innovations instituted by Pune's Mahrattha Chamber of Commerce, Industries & Agriculture (MCCIA) for their Self Retaining Brain Retractor, Sternum Cutting Saw System and Craniotome & Perforator System.

The strength of Madhukar is his innovative ability. He is ready with 3 new products which include e-Drill, e-Saw and Mini Cranitome which are presently undergoing Test Marketing.

Opportunities

His target customers include Orthopedic, Neuro and Cardiac Surgeons. Today, the major share comes from Orthopedic sector. However, the other sectors are catching up fast and fetch a higher price. The present marketing opportunities have been highlighted below:

The market opportunities for original equipments, consumables and repair services look quite substantial. By a rough estimate, around 5,000 surgeons pass out every year from medical colleges in India. The estimated population of surgeons in the country is conservatively estimated at 100, 000.

The number of specialty hospitals in the country is on the rise. The medical tourism in the country is estimated at around Rs. 20, 000 crores per annum.

The world markets offer considerable opportunities. If they are explored in a systematic manner, they can also contribute substantially to the turn over. MSMC has exported to some 20 countries in last 15 years but there is no sustained effort. If done properly, it is possible that more than 50% sales may come from overseas markets, particularly the developing and under developed countries.

Threats

While the opportunities look very bright, there are areas of concern. Some of them have been highlighted below:

A large number of surgeons show a preference towards imported equipments. They are willing to pay a much higher price for the same. The identical looking Chinese products are almost at half the prices of Manman. A section of the market may go for these cheaper products. However, there is a likelihood of poor after-sales service and availability of consumables.

It is difficult to curb the piracy in any field. Many people over the years have started copying Manman products for domestic as well as for overseas markets.

Market size estimation

With inadequate market data available at this stage, it will be difficult to accurately know about the market size. MSMC used the services of a management consultant who came out with the following figures to estimate the market size in India for SPT's.

There are around 100,000 surgeons in the country with

Orthopedic, Neuro and Cardiac specializations.

There are close to 800+ districts in the country. It can be safely assumed that there will be at least 4 hospitals in a town. At least one will be the government hospital. Most of the surgeons will be attached to one or the other hospitals in these districts.

On an average, a surgeon will need surgical power tools worth Rs. 10,000 per year excluding the consumables and repair services. This will be considered as Per Capita Consumption (PCC) for surgical power tools in India.

The export demand for original equipments will be in addition to the domestic demand. This can be conservatively estimated at 50% of the domestic demand per annum.

It can be approximated that 10% revenue can be generated every year from the consumables and repair services respectively of that of the sale of original equipments.

Based on these assumptions, the market size estimation will look as follows:

o   Demand for original surgical power tools: 100,000 numbers x Rs.10,000/- per annum = Rs. 100 crores

o   Demand for consumables (10% of OE demand) = Rs.10 crores

o   Demand for servicing (10% of OE demand) = Rs.10 crores

On the basis of these assumptions, the present market size is estimated at Rs.120 crores per annum. With increase in population, number of surgeons and increase in medical tourism, we can anticipate a growth of 20% per annum on a year to year basis.

The likely market size by 2016 cumulatively is therefore estimated as follows:

Domestic demand Rs.300 crores

Export potential   Rs.150 crores

Total   Rs.450 crores

Competition

The main competition comes from foreign brands. The major names include Stryker (American), Synthes and Linvatec. MSMC quality is not only on par but in some cases superior. This has been seen from the foreign equipments coming to them for repairs. At the same time, the prices of MSMC are lower by 50-60% and more. This makes Manman the most popular brand in surgical power tools in India. Few other local manufacturers mostly in small scale sector enter the market but lack sustainability. Many are copying Manman designs.

Some other problems

Besides the family trauma faced by Madhukar, he was under strain on account of following factors:

Madhukar is a father figure to his staff. Few unscrupulous workers took advantage of his nature. They tried to create problems by disturbing the relations amongst workers. At one moment, Madhukar felt like closing his business. However, under instructions from his labor consultant, he made these trouble makers leave the organization. Madhukar himself had to undergo a by-pass surgery few years back. It cannot be denied that age is catching.

He has close relations with most of his clients all over the country. Many are supplied products without taking care of commercial aspects. This creates problems of high debtors.

Presently, he has 40 dealers across the country. Most of them are working with MSMC since beginning. They also take their sweet time in making payments.

Madhukar is basically an Innovator. He cannot be said to be very strong in commercial aspects. He has developed close to 10 new products which are in various stages of development. The R & D is almost looked after by him single handedly. The gestation period ranges from 2-4 years. If this can be shortened, the company can reap rich dividends.

Planning for the future

Lately, Madhukar has been thinking of the future. He knows for sure that there is a bright potential for the company. He also nurtures ambition to make Manman a global brand. The question is how to go about it?

Some options which he has to consider are as follows:

o Sell the business to an established and big organization. Even though no valuation has been done, he knows that looking at the strengths of MSMC; he can get a substantial sum and enjoy his retirement. However, this does not meet his entrepreneurial spirit.

o Develop a professional organization by hiring talented managers and giving the reins in their hands while still keeping the ownership with him.

o Groom the existing manpower and make them take bigger responsibilities. The question of Succession Planning also needs to be given due consideration.

o Prepare a sound long term plan for next 5 years and raise the resources. This will include creating a strong marketing organization, a large dealer network across the country and also going after the exports in a big way.

This is the classic story of a successful entrepreneur. He has blown the myth that in order to be successful, age, gender, education, experience and money is not at all important. What you require is only passion, ethics and a confidence in yourself. Now he nurtures the ambition to make it big in domestic as well as global markets. What advice would you give to him?

Premium Chick Feeds Private Limited (PCFPL)

Shirish Bhalwankar was making a passionate plea on the occasion of their annual meet. This was their 20th year and as such a land mark year. The meeting was being attended by around 15 persons, which included his three partners, heads of departments and seven regional managers.

'We have done well in last 20 years reaching a turnover close to Rs.250 crores year ended March 31, 2011. However, I still feel that we are not visible as yet and lack brand equity. The poultry industry in India offers considerable opportunities. We will have to become a more professional organization to tap them. We will have to shed our image of a rural industry and come out with a strategic plan for growth. I feel confident that if done systematically, we can easily reach a turnover of Rs.1000 crore by 2020. In this ambitious venture, I solicit your enthusiastic support'.

Poultry Industry in India

India with its present population of 121 crores and growing at 1.6% per annum offers tremendous potential to poultry industry. By a rough estimate, the population comprises equally of vegetarian and non-vegetarians. Amongst, non-vegetarians, almost 90% show preference to poultry products because of its afford ability and availability. The potential can further be gauged from the fact that the present per capita consumption of eggs in India is only 53 and that of poultry meat at 3.2 kgs as against the level recommended by National Institute of Nutrition (NIN) of 180 eggs and 11 kg of poultry meat, respectively. Processing of poultry production is presently at a low rate of 2 % due to lack of processing facilities, cold chains and retail infrastructure.

The Government of India has provided packages for encouraging and stimulating the development of poultry and hatchery industry. The poultry industry provides direct and indirect employment to over 32 lakh persons. Little over 2 crores agricultural farmers, especially the maize and soya growers, are also dependent for their livelihood on poultry industry. This is because 75-80% of the cost of production in the poultry industry consists of feed ingredients like maize and soya.

The poultry industry in India has the inherent strength and resilience to face the challenges in the form of high prices of feed ingredients and increase in input costs.

A SWOT analysis of the poultry industry gives the following picture.

Opportunities

There is distant increase in the consumption of poultry products. A new breed of Eggatarians has emerged in the country. The consumption of Table Chicken is also on the rise with preferential taste for dressed chicken.

The traditional vegetarian markets like Gujarat and some pockets of South India are increasing the consumption of poultry products.

The younger generation in the country is opting for fast food of poultry products with the rise of chains like Mc Donald's, KFC, Pizza Hut, Dominos and others.

There is an increase in the eating out habits of Indian consumers with the rise of mid-range budget hotels and specialty restaurants.

With urbanization, the market for dressed chicken (ready-to cook) and value-added (ready-to-eat) is on the rise.

Organized food retail is booming like hyper city, Spencer's and others.

Threats

There is periodic grain shortage in the industry pressurizing feed production, catalyzed by inflation and fluctuating overheads.

Seasonal viral and bacterial diseases affecting productivity.

Increased intense competition from huge capital players, ready to spend cash reserves on farming markets.

Over production with minimum room for differentiation, resulting into long-term price backlash.

Seasonality due to intense summer in several parts of the country as well as religious beliefs in certain months there by affecting the demand.

The major players

It is interesting to note that the industry is dominated mostly by local players. When it comes to parent stocks, breeders and hatcheries, Pune's Venkateshwara Hatcheries Limited is the giant. Started by Dr. B. V. Rao who is considered as the father of modern poultry industry in India, they are almost in every field including poultry vaccines, processed poultry products and also the fast food outlets under the name of Venky's express. They are giving tough competition to foreign outlets like McDonalds and KFC. Their annual turnover is in excess of Rs. 5000 crores per annum. Another big name in poultry is Suguna Chicken whose turnover is around Rs.3500 crores per annum. The leader in feed manufacturing is Godrej Agrovet. Except for an Indonesian company names Japfa and CP, foreign names are almost missing in Indian markets. The overall poultry industry in India is worth Rs.37000 crores per annum growing at 10% per annum. There are around 250,000 poultry farmers across the country where Market Logistics plays a major role.

History of PCFPL

It is interesting to find that four persons, comparatively with different backgrounds and temperament came together to start the business as partners in April 1991. They are,

Dr. Shirish Bhalwankar (MVSc& AH): Poultry Expert in Production, Technical, Quality Control

Dr. Ram Bhuwan (BVSc& AH): Poultry Expert in Technical, Business Development, Administration

Mr. Tarun Baheti (BCom): Agro Stockist& Trader Finance, Purchase, Procurement

Mr. Phil Fagrado (BSc): Agro Stockist & Trader, Projects, Maintenance

Mr. Tarun Baheti decided to withdraw from the partnership in August 2012 as he was keen on developing his business as a Builder. It is heartening to note that their association has strengthened over the years and the conflicts are almost non-existent. However, there is one more concern they will have to attend to in near future. That is of succession planning. All the partners are now in the age group of 50 to 60. Their children, with the exception of the daughter of Ram Bhuwan, are not very enthusiastic about joining the family business. Revati, daughter of Ram has recently joined five year course for Bachelors in Veterinary Science (BVSc.). There is no guarantee that after the completion of the course whether she will be interested in joining PCFPL.

PCFPL started as a feed manufacturer. However, they felt that the opportunities are more in poultry integration. A second organization under the name of Premier Hatchery Private Limited was set up. As such, it can be considered that there are two SBU's under the Premier group, namely for feed manufacturing and for poultry integration. There is no separate organization structure and the ownership also remains the same.

Organization structure

There is no formal organization structure. All the directors are involved in all activities. Generally there is no conflict. However, it is felt that a proper organization structure needs to be defined with duties & responsibilities.

What does PCFPL do?

The PCFPL is in the business of Integrated Broiler Production. The product mix comprises of the following:

Breeding: Farming of Parent / Grandparent birds

Production: Production of breed chicks supplied to poultry farmers

Nutrition: Manufacture of quality chicken feed for sale to poultry farmers

Farming: Engaging poultry farmers on buyback model

Distribution: Collection and Supply of birds to markets through traders

Present capacities

The present capacities of PCFPL can be enumerated as given below:

Hi-tech Pelletised Feed Plants: 3.5 acres at Poynad (Raigad) – 8,000 - 10,000 tonnes per month, plus on term contract in Bhiwandi (Thane) and Narayangaon (Pune).

State-of-the-art Chick Hatchery 6 acres at Poynad (Raigad) – plus on term contract in Bhiwandi, Wada, Kalyan, Dahanu (Thane), Vani (Nasik) and Murud (Raigad). 5,00,000 + hatch per week.

Spread of PCFPL

Parent Breeding Farm 1 Lakh sq.ft.at Kamshet (Pune) 60,000 breeders plus 1, 20,000 breeders on integration at Mudbagal and Palamner (Karnataka) (Karnataka) and 70 ,000 breeders in Lonand (Satara)

Commercial Broiler Farms (under Integration) 2000 Commercial Broiler Farms with capacities ranging 2000 - 20,000 chicks per farm primarily spread over the Konkan (Thane, Raigad, Ratnagiri) & Western Maharashtra (Nasik, Pune, Satara) region

Market input of PCFPL

o 22 lakh chicks per month is placement in the integration model.

o 21 lakh birds per month is minimum supply with mortality controlled at 4 per cent

o 55 lakhs birds per week is aggregate supply to the MMR market (1.6 kg -1.8 kg avg. wt.)

The present market share of PCFPL is 11 %, almost every 8thbird consumed in the Mumbai Metropolitan Region (MMR)belongs to them.

Present market coverage

Location Distribution of Premium Commercial Broiler Farms:

Pune   30%

Raigad   35%

Thane, Nasik   35%

Market flow

The present and proposed market flows of PCFPL are given below:

Current value chain

Chick Supplier & Feed Vendor (PCF) – Farmer – Integrator (PCF) – Trader – Retailer – Consumer

Proposed value chain

Chick Supplier & Feed Vendor (PCF) – Farmer – Integrator (PCF) – Processor (PCF) – Stockiest (PCF) – Retailer

Past Performance

The graph below shows the sales performance over last 10 years. The appendix gives the Balance Sheet and the Profit & Loss statement for the year ended March 31, 2011.

The future and growth strategies

'We are not sure how we should plan our future. Should we grow in feed business or in poultry integration? Each one has several threats as well as opportunities. Should we also consider diversification in non-core area? We have aspirations. We would also like to go global but how we do not know? We want to build Premium brand and may plan an IPO in the future. I do not know whether we will be able to attract funds from public? How do we chalk our growth strategy? 'Concluded Dr. Bhalwankar.

The sales performance for last 5 years and the latest Balance Sheet is given in the appendix.

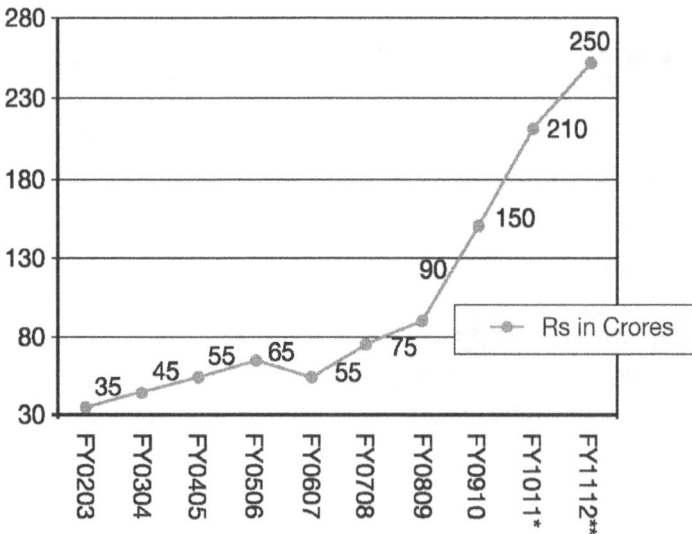

PREMIUM CHICK FEEDS PVT LTD

AT - TADWAGLE, POST-POYNAD,
TAL - ALIBAG, DIST - RAIGAD
BALANCE SHEET AS --- MARCH 31.2011

PARTICULARS	Sch No.	As at 31.03.2011	As at 31.05.2010
SOURCES ON FUNDS			
SHAREHOLDERS' FUND			
Share Capital	1	15,000.000.00	15,000,000.00
Reserve and Surplus	2	62,802.865.02	31,049,311.90
		87,802.855.02	46,049,311.90
LOAN FUNDS			
Secured Loans	3	68,003.127.05	61,907,774,33
Unsecured Loans	4	4,350.000.00	1,250,000,03
		70,353,127.05	62,257,774,33
Deferred Tax Liability's	4A	825,832.48	1,035,828,57
		138,981,864.55	109,342,912,80
TOTAL			
APPLICATION OF FUNDS	5		
FIXED ASSETS		90,259.280.00	87.820,154,00
Gross Block		40,016,704.61	33,743,620,52
Accumulated Depreciation		50,242,578.39	34,075,573,39
Net Block			
	6		
INVESTMENTS			
	7		
CURRENT ASSETS LOANS & ADVANCES		23,526,904.25	76,689,746,34
Inventor as	8	00,310,901,85	127,996,031,21
Sundry Debtors	9	30.490,501.55	10,022,526,18
Cash and Bank Balances	A	18.385,853.00	19,802,688,66
Loans & Advances		272,713,340.60	243,010,794,38
Current Liabilities & Provisions			
Current Liabilities	10	84,381,652.49	146,266,297,57
Provision	11	19.592,192.00	2,976,157,00
	B	183,074,054,40	158,281,454,87
NET CURRENT ASSETS	(A+B)	88,739,286.16	75,208,339,41
MISC. EXPENSES	12		
TOTAL		138,981,664.66	109,342,912,10

Coalfields of India Ltd. (COIL)

Changeover from sellers market to buyer's market.

COIL was set up in the year 1971 when all the coking coal mines were nationalized by Govt. of India. Except for the captive mines of TISCO AND IISCO, all the mines are now owned by Central Government. COIL was formed as a holding company which has nine subsidiaries under it.

Moving with the times, the top management felt that all the managers must be imparted continuous training in different areas of management. A training institute was set up at Ranchi in Bihar (Now in Zarkhand). It was called Coalfields Institute of Management (CIM). No efforts were spared to make it one of the grandest institutes in the country. It was set up over an area of 100 acres by spending around Rs. 25 Crores IN 1996. The Infrastructure developed was A class with five star facilities for participants as well as the faculty. The institute was inaugurated by the President of India on July 1, 1996. The institute had an Executive Director (ED) who reported directly to the Chairman of COIL. He started work with a skeleton staff. He found it difficult to get the faculty both on permanent as well as visiting basis mainly because of their location.

It was decided that for the first year, three premier management development institutes would be invited to conduct six programmes each. The meeting was called by the executive director with the representatives of the management institutes to design a module of ten days each.

Said the ED, 'By and large I agree with the design of the course which you have proposed except for two days you have allotted to study of Marketing. COIL does not require any Marketing. We have monopoly in COAL extraction and distribution. We are not selling soaps, soft drinks or TV Sets. The representatives tried to reason with the ED the need to study marketing. They emphasized that particularly after the liberalization; no organization can take such a stand so as to ignore marketing. However, ED was adamant. So as not to lose business opportunities, all the institutes agreed to exclude the study of marketing in the MDP.

Coal Sector in India

Almost 60 percent of the total electricity generated in India comes from Thermal Power where coal is a major feed stock. Coal is also used in different industries for their processes and energy requirements. The consumption of coal by railways is on the decline. Even then, they are the major customers of COIL. Table 1 gives the consumption of coal by major user sectors.

Table 1 : Coal consumption in India (%)

Secto	%
Electricity boards	62.6
Steel Plants	10.9
Railways	01.6
Fertilizer	01.9
Cement	04.6
Soft Coke Manufacturing	00.3
Brick Kilns, Chemicals, Textile, Paper & Others	16.5
Captive Consumption	01.5
Exports	00.1
Total	100.0

During the year 2010-11, the production of coal registered a level of 430 million tones. The growth rates over the years were marginal at 3-5 per cent per annum. The imports of coal which was not permitted earlier had started increasing after the liberalization. For 2010-11, it was at around 100 million tones registering a growth of almost 80% over the earlier years.

A separate organization was set up in 1992 to look after the distribution and quality control of coal. It was called Controller of Coals (CC). However, this organization whose staff was drawn from the subsidiaries of COIL lacked teeth.

The subsidiaries continued to operate in the same fashion as they did since nationalization. That means, they hardly bothered to deliver the coal on time and of quality. The customers regularly complained as to why they should pay for the stones supplied along with coal by COIL companies. At times, this percentage was as high as 30 per cent. However, none of the users could take any drastic action against COIL. Its monopoly was strong and fearsome. Some of the genuine complaints of the user sectors were as below:

o They never received promised delivery on time. At times, they faced emergency situation of having only a week's coal stock or so. COIL always refused to acknowledge the blame passing it on to Railways for shortage of wagons and delays in delivery.

o The quality of coal was always poor. This reduced the efficiency of their own performance and occasionally created problems of malfunctioning of the machinery.

o The users other than the government sector had to pay the money in advance there by blocking the funds and creating problems for working capital management. COIL refused to accept this charge. On the contrary, they complained about the high level of debtors they have to carry particularly on account of Railways and some state electricity boards.

o Most of the users found the behavior of COIL staff high handed. Not only they were rude, they expected bribes before dispatches can be made.

With the monopoly which COIL enjoyed, how was their

financial performances? Were they making profit? This was not to be and most of the subsidiaries, barring one or two were always in the red. COIL had accumulated losses of the order of Rs. 1700 crores. The government had decided to either write them off or convert the debts in equity.

COIL came out with a public issue in 2011 which changed its fortune. With accumulated losses written off, large funds in the kitty through IPO, suddenly COIL was rolling in money. For some time, they had the highest market cap in the stock market. But, did it changed its culture and outlook towards the customer?

COIL had its hand full with problems. They included:

- Surplus manpower. Roughly, 30 per cent of its manpower amounting to around 70,000 employees was considered surplus.

- The several unions, all affiliated to various political parties, were highly militant. They stoutly opposed any scheme to reduce the manpower.

- In several mines, 'mafia raj' prevailed. Stealing of coal, beating of COIL officers and other such threats continued.

Some latest data from COIL gives an impressive picture as given below:

- COIL. is a Maharatna Company with net worth of Rs. 33,314 Crores as on 31.3.11 and profit after tax Rs. 10,867 Crores in 2010-2011.

- It is the largest coal producing company in the world.

It contributed about 81% of total Coal production in India.

- As of March 31, 2011 COIL operates 471 mines spread over in eight states out of which 273 are underground, 163 opencast and 35 mixed mines and it operates 17 Coal Beneficiation Plants. CIL produces both coking and non - coking coal.

- During 2010-2011, COIL produced 431.32 million tonnes of coal.

- COIL employees strength consists of 3,71,546 permanent employees including 18,384 (as on 01.04.12) executives and has its headquarter at Kolkata, West Bengal.

The major question the faculty has to address while conducting the MDP was how to change the mind set of COIL managers, right from top to bottom. The Chairman & Managing Director of COIL normally came up from the ranks and had an average stay of 2 years or less. When an incumbent came, he was very powerful. Most of the times, dictated by the political bosses, they never bothered to bring any radical changes. 'The paradigm shift' was a terminology unheard of at COIL. Can they learn something from their counterparts from abroad? The coal industry in U.K. also is in a monopolistic situation. However, as per reports received, they have understood the importance of Marketing. Periodically, they carry out customer satisfaction measurement surveys and act on it. Will such a thing ever happen at COIL?

In the changed scenario of LPG (Liberalization, Privatization and Globalization) how long will COIL be able to continue in the same manner? Will they and when they will discover Marketing?

Some of the aspects which needed urgent attention of COIL were as follows:

- Discuss in details why COIL should change their orientation?

- How should they go about it? Identify any other companies from public or private sector who are yet to discover Marketing. Why?

Apex Electrical Company Ltd.

Mr. Nathan, Sales Manager of Apex Electrical Co. Ltd. had just received a proposal from his Regional Manager at Bangalore for opening a sub-office in Madras and was considering what would be the best decision in the company's short term as well as long term interest.

The Company was in the business of manufacturing and marketing electric motors of a wide range of horse power that could be used as a prime mover in numerous applications. The company's factory and head office were situated in Bombay and it had its branch offices at New Delhi, Calcutta and Bangalore, each headed by a Regional Manager.

The Regional Office at Bangalore was responsible for sales in Karnataka, Tamil Nadu and Kerala. The company also maintained a godown at Bangalore which was used as the stocking centre for feeding sales in the complete region. The company's distribution network had grown over several years and as such there was no one rule by which the arrangements could be explained. In Karnataka, due to the proximity of the Regional Head Quarters, the distribution network was closely controlled by the Regional Office. Company had several dealers covering the State and they all purchased goods directly from the Regional Office. All the dealers got got a fixed percentage of discounts. The ultimate prices to the consumers were fixed by the company. Each dealer covered a specific area which was generally one to several districts and the company discouraged one dealer interfering in other's territory. However, in main cities of Bangalore and Mysore, there were more than one dealer who collectively covered the sales in the city. The company salesman regularly contacted the dealers and the office maintained good marketing information.

In states of Tamil Nadu and Kerala, However, the arrangement was quite different. Due to some historical reasons, all the sales in this territory were channeled through one single distributor. This distributor in turn had appointed his own dealers to cover the cities of Madras and Cochin and other districts of the two States. The Regional Office, therefore, had very little information on the exact marketing set up in this territory and the distributor operated almost independently. On several occasions, the Regional Manager had attempted to bring the distributor under his closer control. He had an impression that company was not able to exploit the full potential of the region due to the authoritarian rule of the distributor. He had occasional reports that the distributor was not even aware of certain important tenders floated in the region and on other occasions, he had not bothered to submit quotations in time. There were also complaints received from some of the dealers that they did not get a fair deal and would instead prefer to deal with the company directly. Sales and service personnel of the Regional Office used to visit the States of

Tamil Nadu and Kerala only when requested specifically by the distributor as it would mean by passing him. The real reason behind this was that the distributor had in the initial stages given considerable financial help to the company. He was also an important shareholder and thus had connections at the highest level. This did not mean the top management was prepared to sacrifice company's interests, but otherwise, they preferred to leave the distributor undisturbed.

The Regional Manager felt that the little pieces of negative feed back he had received could be the tip of an iceberg. However, in the absence of concrete information, he could never put up a convincing case against the distributor. He had always been helpless whenever some dealers working under the distributor complained to him. He felt it would seriously affect their morale if they realized the company could not control the distributor.

He had discussed this matter at length with the Sales Manager Mr. Nathan who realized some tight-rope walking was needed if he had to steer clear of this problem. Mr. Nathen was, however, anxious to do something about it and one idea was to open an office at Madras, the head quarters of the distributor. While this would be for the declared purpose of helping the distributor in marketing efforts, it would also put an automatic check on undesirable practices. Moreover the sub-office can collect more factual information that could be used to put up a convincing case against the distributor if such a need arose. Accordingly, the Regional Manager how now submitted a detailed proposal for opening a sub-office at Madras which would look after Tamil Nadu to start with.

The Company had a strict policy of insisting on the regional office to achieve a fixed ratio of sales per rupee of expenses. For the Bangalore Office this ratio of sales per rupee of expenses. For the Bangalore Office this ratio was 50 in the previous year when the sales were Rs. 12 cr. and expenses Rs. 24 Lakhs. Of this, the sales in Tamil Nadu were Rs. 3 Cr.

The proposal stated a sales forecast of Rs. 3.5 cr. in Tamil Nadu in next year and estimated expenses of Madras sub-office at Rs. 7 lakhs, thus achieving a ratio of Rs. 50 sales per rupee of expense. Among other things, the details of the proposal stated under split up of the expenses Rs. 2.3 lakhs toward salary and Rs. 1.75 lakhs toward travelling expenses of two sales personnel who would be transferred from Bangalore to Madras.

Questions :

- What decision would you take if you were in place of Mr. Nathan?

- Do you feel the proposal of new sub-office is economically justified against the stated policy of the company? If yes, why? If no, then how could it be made justifiable?

Industrial Valves Ltd.

It is said that many a business deals are made in social functions, clubs, etc. Mr. Khanna, Chief Executive of Industrial Valves Ltd. was having a hearty chat with Mr. Dhavan, Chief Executive of U.P. Chemicals at Delhi Club over a glass of beer. The latter asked if IVL could supply immediately 20 stainless steel gate valves of 250 mm size for their dyestuff plant within two weeks. Mr. Khanna gave an assurance that there will be no problem in giving the delivery.

Next morning, Mr. Khanna called his sales manager Mr. Sood and told that this particular commitment must be fulfilled as he has given his word. The sales manager agreed to do the needful. For Northern India, they had appointed V. K. Engineers as their main distributors. Mr. Sood called the distributors to check if they can give any delivery from their stocks. When informed that they did not have any stocks of the valves required, he checked the production programme. Some 30 valves of that type were ready for dispatch to some other party and the next lot was scheduled after another 4 weeks. He took a decision to divert the dispatches to U.P. Chemicals under advice to their distributors

V.K. Engineers who got their commission on all orders executed in their territory.

Mr. Khanna and Mr. Dhavan met again at the club after about 10 days since their last meeting and the latter profusely complimented Mr. Khanna for such a prompt supply. He also mentioned that within a year their expansion plan would require a large number of valves and IVL would be the obvious choice for the supplies.

The Valves worked well for four months and then one of them was found leaking. The service engineer complained to the plant manager who in turn wrote a letter promptly to Industrial Valves Ltd. They got a reply that the service is looked after by their dealer. VK Engineers and they would do the needful. After three more requests, a service engineer of the dealer called on the factory and inspected the defective valve. He pointed out that it's a design defect and there is nothing he can do. As such, they better refer the matter to the manufacturers. During this time, six more valves had started leaking and no corrective action was taken either by the manufacturer or the dealer. The production of UP Chemicals was getting hampered and only temporary repairs could be made. With the result, when the enquiries were floated by UP Chemicals for valves for their expansion project. Industrial Valves ltd. was totally ignored.

When Mr. Khanna came to know of this, he was furious. He felt that the time has come when he must evaluate the effectiveness of his dealer network. And if required, he should add or delete some.

Questions :

- Whom would you blame for the above situation and why?

- Discuss the role of the dealer / distributor in marketing of industrial goods.

- How would you carry out the study on the effectiveness of channels of distribution?

Hercules Heavy Engineering Corporation

Transportation of oversize dimensional consignment (ODC)

As against the trend towards miniaturization for electronic and electrical goods, large scale economies come into play for production of cement, fertilizers, electricity, etc. As the capital cost is distributed over a larger production, the unit cost of production goes down. However, this has developed several other problems besides the availability of technical know-how, manufacturing and testing facilities for these equipments.

Mr. Rakesh Sood, General Sales Manager of Hercules Heavy Engineering Corporation has a curious problem facing him. For the first time, they quoted for cement plants with capacity of 3500 tonnes per day. They have grabbed three orders from three corners of India, one each near Kanpur, Trichirapalli and Jaipur. With their Swiss collaboration, technical know-how is no problem. With their excellent facilities at Bhor, 50 Kms. from Poona, they are in a position to manufacture and test the goods. What is worrying them right from today is after completion of the plant, how to ship it to these different sites?

Each plant comprises of around 100 sub-assemblies. There are only 10-12 sub-assemblies which could be considered as critical with maximum dimensions and weights as below:

- Max. dia. 6 metres.

- Max. weight 70 tonnes

- Length of largest Piece 17 metres.

The customer is going to pay for the transportation cost. However, the mode of transportation, route, delivery,cost, insurance etc. has to be decided by the manufacturer. There are agencies who are in the business of ODC Transport. However, this size of consignment has not been handled by any one of them before. A scientific study and planning is, therefore, desired so that the experience would be of use to others faced with similar situations.

Questions :

- Discuss the alternatives available for physical distribution from all angles.

- List out the operations to be performed in a systematic manner till the time the plant reaches the site.

Jackson India Ltd.

Demotivated or incompetent?

Mr. Mudliar, the Marketing Manger of Jackson India was extremely concerned about the performance of his Regional managers during last one year and was wondering if there was something terribly wrong with his staff.

Jackson India was formerly a foreign company incorporated in Calcutta for the manufacture of Sheet Metal Containers. Immediately after the independence, however, it was taken over by a large Indian group. The company was one of the pioneers in the country in the field of Metal Containers and enjoyed a virtual monopoly in the market for several years. It was only during last 10 years that competition had been steadily getting tougher and tougher and during last two years the Company's sales had actually dropped from their peak level of Rs. 200 crores to 60 crores.

The Company's head office was in Calcutta from where the Marketing Manager controlled all the marketing activities. The Company had 8 regional offices including one in Calcutta which together covered the entire market in the country. Each regional office was headed by a Regional manager who had Sales Engineers working under him. The regional offices also had their own accounts and stores departments to handle the other supporting functions. The regional offices were completely independent of HO in their day-to-today workings. Each regional office had one godown attached where standard metal container stocks were maintained.

Most of the present Regional Managers had been with the Company for past 15 to 20 years and had come up from the ranks. At least 3 of them had started their careers with he Company as stenographers or stores assistant and built themselves to the present level. The Company had a policy of encouraging people from within and this had indeed provided ample growth opportunities for its employees as can be seen from the cases of Regional Managers. The loyalty and integrity of all these managers was beyond doubt as most of them had made their careers in the Company.

The salaries drawn were very much competitive which similar size companies offered. During the first two decades after independence, the company had enjoyed the monopoly in the market and the Regional Managers had shown exceptional performance, winning turnover and incentive prizes year after year. The setting in of competition was however something the Company and its managers were not prepared for. During the last few years, the managers had seen many of their old customers lost and had not been able to do any things about it.

Mr. Mudliar was aware of the limitations within which a Marketing Manager could show his mettle. If the Company's products had become incompetive, no manager would be able to sell them unless some revision of prices was done at the highest level.

But what worried Mr. Mudliar most was the almost total loss of control on sales that the Regional Managers were showing in several of their actions. With growing competition, it had become necessary for the regional offices to show more alertness about grabbing marketing opportunities. He expected them to rush to him with problems of pricing and deliveries. But nothing like that was happening. It was as if no manager was bothered whether the Company sales went up or down.

Mr. Mudliar had lately introduced a detailed reporting system for the regional offices. The idea was to make them concentrate their attention on key variables of sales, stocks and outstandings and get a regular review of the situation made. Very few of them, however, had been punctual in sending the reports. And even those who sent them had written such meaningless collection of stray data that Mr. Mudliar had serious doubts whether they had understood even 1% of their real responsibilities.

Day by day, Mr. Mudliar was getting an impression that his managers were good when it was a sweet job of rationing the monopoly products. But, they just did not know what marketing in a competitive market really is. And it was a frightening thought that not even one of his team of ten managers was any good for the challenges of the time.

Some of the senior colleagues of Mr. Mudliar felt differently about it. They did agree that over the years, some kind of lethargy had come over the Regional Managers. But they did not believe that the managers were incompetent. Instead, they felt that the managers saw no more scope for advancement as there was only one position of Marketing Manager. As such, they were frustrated. Moreover, through the new information system established recently, they had felt a loss of autonomy and this had lead to a kind of non-cooperation which was not intentional. 'Incompetent or Demotivated is the real question' thought Mr. Mudliar and a lot depended upon what the answer was. In the meanwhile, the decline continued and for the first time in its history, TIL was to report a whooping loss.

Questions :

- What do you feel could be the real reason behind this problem?

- What remedial actions will you suggest for Jackson India?

GL Diesels Limited

The production of diesel engines in India is upto the rating of 2000 horse power. The market is dominated by two giants, one catering from 5 hp to 400 hp range and the another company from 200 hp to 2000 hp. Range. Thus, when GL diesels decided to enter the market for diesel engines, they decided that they would concentrate on the range upto 20 hp. Only. As against the total production of around 6 lakh engines in the country coming from something like 500 manufacturers, almost 60% market share is for engines below 20 hp. This is in terms of quantity. Surprisingly, there are hardly thirty manufacturers of diesel engines who are in the organized sector.

GL Diesels Ltd. was set up at Ahmednagar in Maharashtra, a notably backward district. It was with Italian collaboration. It was claimed that these engines are with low weight, high speed and high efficiency. As such, they should be welcome by the Indian customers as it would have given them a lower fuel consumption for performing the same work. The prices also could be lower marginally.

The licensed capacity of the factory was 100,000

engines. The production commenced on 1st August 1980.

In this range of diesel engines, the applications are very clearly defined. The major share being in the agricultural sector. This could be for operating a pump set, for running a mill and other sundry operations. Some market also is available for diesel gensets which are used by touring theatres, cinema houses, et.

As such it will be seen that the market is very large in terms of geographic coverage. The company had hired in Mr. Anand an able marketing manager. He had considerable experience in the marketing of diesel engines having worked with the other, major manufacturer. The company had yet to develop a distribution setup. The sale department was also not organized properly. In the first six months of its operations, the company had manufactured and sold 10,000 diesel engines.

Mr. Anand was thinking seriously about the total setup for the marketing on the whole and sales department in particular. Sooner he does it, he will be in a better position to get a substantial share of the large market.

Questions :

- How would you design the sales organization for this company?

- What should be the ideal sales force size for this company in your opinion?

- How would you do the territory design?

Rast Frit Steel Foundry

Rast Frit in Swedish means stainless steel. This name was thus particularly given to this foundry, a subsidiary of Excel Engineering Corporation. The parent company with more than fifty years of history behind has diversified activities in engineering lines covering pumps, valves, diesel engines, electric motors, controls, etc. Some fifteen years back when it was noticed that production at times gets hampered due to delayed supplies or poor quality of castings; it was decided that a separate foundry will be set up to mainly cater to the captive requirements. As such, Rast Frit Steel Foundry was set up at Ahmednagar, 112 Km. from Pune where the main factory of the parent company is located.

The performance of Rast Frit over the years could be considered quite satisfactory. Starting with the initial capacity of 8000 tons per annum, the capacity was increased to 12000 tons per annum in the year 1990. The years from 1989 to 1992 when recession in the engineering industry affected the parent company, were trying years for Rast Frit too. It was then realized by the management that too much dependence on the parent company would be harmful. More sales efforts were then made to get orders from other units which were quite successful. Today, the order book on an average shows 30% workload from the parent company and the balance from outside customers. In terms of materials of casting, in spite of the name, cast iron constituted 90% of the production while the balance goes for alloy steel castings. The facilities available covering care making, melting, fettling, shot blasting, testing, etc. are quite modern. The present level of production reached is around 10,000 tons per annum. Looking at the bright potential for various types of castings, the company has applied to Government of India for an additional capacity of 12000 tons per annum. As no foreign technical know-how or import of machinery is involved, it is most likely that this expansion will be sanctioned.

Today, in 1996-97 Rast Frit is catering to such prestigious clients like Heavy Vehicles Factory, Bajaj Auto Ltd; TELCO; Kirloskar Tractors, Premier Automobiles, etc. and has a turnover of Rs. 2,000 million per annum. In December 1995, a Japanese Team visited India. It was looking for suppliers of castings all over the world. They visited Rast Frit and had a good impression. However, their requirement was around 5000 tons per month which was far beyond their capacity and hence no further follow up was made. This was perhaps for the first time that the management realized about the vast potential for the exports of castings.

In May 1996, the Managing Director of Rast Frit attended the annual function of the Indian Institute of Foundrymen at Calcutta. The President of the organization harped on the theme of 'export of castings.' He regretted that India today is exporting different types of casting worth only Rs. 500 crores per annum as against a potential of around 5000 crores.

The Chairman of the parent company during one of his visits to USA met the President of The Casting Manufacturers Association. During his talks, he noted following things :

The rise in wages abroad, especially in the foundry industry has made the cost of manufacturing castings very high.

In developed countries, the workers are shying away from hard jobs, rough conditions, heat etc., in a foundry and hence they have to turn to developing countries for the supply of castings. In USA, the labour rate of a foundry workers was $ 20 per hour.

In the year 1994-95, USA alone imported different types of castings worth 800 US million dollars.

With low labour rates, excellent prospects exit for export of castings from India. The only areas to be watched would be quality, keeping the rejection rate low and maintaining deliveries.

Upon his return to India, the Chairman set up a separate cell to plan the operations for the export of castings to developed countries.

Questions :

• With such a vast potential prevailing for export of castings, why the Indian foundries have not come forward and exploited the opportunities?

- As the first step in planning a strategy, it was decided to undertake a market research project. How will you carry out this project and what type of data would you require for planning it?

- How would you plan the marketing strategy for this company?

Switchgears and Controls Ltd.

Legal aspects of marketing

The favorite joke of Mr. Venkar Ramani, Marketing Manager of S & C Ltd., after reviewing any new technical documentation of the company products used to be, "See, you have again given the dimensions in inches and weights in pounds. So if anybody sues as under the weights & measures act, let us decide who will go to the jail." The promotion manager, Mr. Murthy whose job it was to look after the preparation of the complete documentation and Mr. Ramani usually used to laugh it over. The documentation included sales & technical literature, instruction manuals, foundation details and price lists. The fact was that the production department who had got all their drawings from U.K. were still using the F.P.S. System.

The Company was manufacturing starters, relays, switch fuse units, circuit-breakers, etc. When the company had started at Madras in 1956, the technical know-how was obtained from a well-known British Company. At least two recent happenings made Mr. Ramani look at the matter more seriously. A terse letter was received from Indian Standards Institute asking for an explanations to why they have not yet switched over to the MKS System.

The second issue was even more critical. For last one year or so, the company was negotiating with a Finnish Company to obtain the knowhow for a superior quality miniature circuit breaker. Two engineers of S & S Ltd. had even received two months training at Helsinki. A prototype was developed at Madras. However, at the last minute, an agreement on the fees could not be reached. Thus, S & C Ltd. had decided to introduce the product in the market on its own. Accordingly, the promotion department had prepared the documentation as well as the advertising plans. This was then introduced in the market. And now a notice was received from an attorney from Calcutta representing the Finnish Company that S & C Ltd. have copied all diagrams and sketches from the documentation of the former company. This was thus an infringement of the copy-rights act and why legal action should not be taken against them?

Mr. Ramani was wondering whether he should hence forward start hiring law graduates for the marketing department?

Questions :

- What are the different laws with which a marketing executive should be familiar? Both for consumer as well as industrial marketing.

- What action should S & C Ltd. take under the given circumstances?

Dabhol Power Corporation

The Dabhol Power Project – the 80 percent subsidiary of the Houston based Enron Development Corporation makes an interesting case study for the students for any discipline. Seldom we come across a project which is found engulfed in controversies of every kind giving rise to questionable ethical practices. Five years have passed and still there is no end to these controversies. During this time, Enron is always in the news bringing forth many issues confusing all and sundry.

Historical background

July 1991 brought the euphoria of liberalization. The then Congress government painted a picture that now all the problems of the country are over. The License and Inspector Raj will be the thing of the past. All areas of industry barring a handful will now be open for private sector. Foreign companies will be allowed to enter Indian markets and will be permitted to hold equity upto 51 percent and even more with certain conditions. Every thing will be available in plenty. The economic reforms will result in 'Garibi Hatao'. After six years, how many of these promises have been fulfilled?'

Maharashtra State under the Chief Minister ship of Mr. Sharad Pawar was not to lag behind. They wanted to be the first state to cash on the benefits of liberalization. And they chose 'power sector' to begin with. An announcement in early 1993 that Maharashtra State Electricity Board (MSEB) has entered in a power purchase agreement (PPA) with Dabhol Power Company (DPC) to allow the latter to set 695 MW, gas fired power project with a total cost outlay of US $ 920 million surprised many. And the hell was let loose.

The then opposition, a coalition of Bharatiya Janata Party (BJP) and Shiv Sena (SS) fought the forthcoming elections for the State assembly accusing the ruling party of corruption of a large magnitude. Of them, BJP was a more vocal partner. They raised many more objections other than the monetary corruption. The then opposition leader (presently the deputy chief minister of Maharashtra) Mr. Gopinath Mundhe promised to sink the Enron project in the Arabian Sea. They were given all the facts and figures by their BSS sponsored 'think tank', the 'Swadeshi Jagran Manch' led by Mr. S. Gurumurthy. Gullible voters, fed up with stories of corruption and looking for change gave their votes to the coalition. Short of absolute majority, the combine of BJP + SS with the support of independent MLAs formed the next government in Maharashtra. The vociferous Mundhe besides becoming the deputy CM also got the energy ministry. Now the ball was in his court. An enquiry committee under the leadership of Mundhe was set up to probe the Enron contract.

The Mundhe Committee report listed out the following points to recommend scrapping of the project :

The cost of the project was padded by at least 26 percent. The Enron defense was that the country comparisons are not always valid.

DPC was more expensive than other fast track projects. Enron insisted that it was comparable.

The World Bank had advised against it. They felt that the project should not be based on imported gas but should use local coal or gas. Enron defended that the State does not have local coal. Imported coal and gas both cost roughly the same and gas is cleaner.

No competitive bidding was done. Enron defended that at the time the project was awarded, there were very few takers and the policy on bidding was non-existant.

MSEB will go bust as they will have to pay to Enron through their noses. Enron contended that it is upto the efficiency of MSEB in terms of its revenue collections.

The earlier government rushed through giving clearance to Enron. The latter defended that this had to be done as the PPA had a time-frame.

Enron had their internal problems too. Linda Powers, a vice-president of Enron gave a statement before a congressional committee saying that Enron has spend money to provide "-- Indian banks a real and concrete understanding of sound project lending practices, --- that around $ 20 million was spent on educating the Indian people ----". This was seen as an admission of bribery by many.

Scrapping of Enron

On Aug. 3, 1995, Chief Minister Mr. Manohar Joshi finally pulled the plug on Enron. The Maharashtra Government announced that they have decided to cancel the agreement made by MSEB with DPC.

The decision to renege on its contract was the outcome of a complex political process involving a prolonged internal debate within the BJP at the national level as well as complicated political maneuvering between the BJP and SS at the State level. The government's statement came out with the following conclusions:

To scrap the second phase of the project as the MSEB has the right of refusal. The energy ministry and the MSEB will be informed to the effect by the State Government.

The state government will direct DPC to stop work on phase I and the contract stands cancelled.

To make the confusion worse, the MSEB's order to Enron a few days letter was more curiously worded. It instructed Enron to stop work 'as instructed by the Govt. of Maharashtra' almost as if MSEB did not agree with the decision. This could have been true as it was believed that MSEB officials who testified before Mundhe Committee defended the project. There were rumours that the adverse report against Enron was prepared by Swdeshi Jagran Manch. And bureaucrats were not happy with the allegations made against them.

There were five reasons cited for the cancellation of the agreement. They were,

- Lack of competitive bidding.

- Lack of transparency.

- Adverse impact on the environment.

- Unrealistic capital costs.

- Escalating tariff.

Salvaging the situation :

Enron came up with a two-pronged strategy. In public, it went through motions of a legal process to claim damages for the cancellation. In private, they sent 'strong signals' through intermediaries expressing its willingness to renegotiate. The possible areas included lowering the cost of the project using naptha as fuel to bring down the tariff. They also suggested that MSEB take a 30% equity stake. The arbitration route under the terms of PPA would have to be in London under the guidance of the United Nations rule on international arbitration. This was a complicated and time consuming procedure.

Enron and its other two promoters, Bechtel and General Electric prepared to go on war because DPC was a major strategy for them to enter India and safeguard their investments in gas fields in Qatar which were meant to supply the Dabhol Plant. They had to get approval to this project, by hook or crook.

The PPA had a list of conditions under which the project can be terminated by the State Government. This included evidence of kickbacks or wrong doing. Despite all rhetoric, BJP + SS could not come out with any evidence to this effect. The chief minister had to categorically state that he has no intention to set up a committee to enquire into such charges against any specific person/s.

Bureaucrats were particularly disturbed with all these developments. Enron was invited to India by a group of senior ones including the then power secretary S. Rajgopal. He was heralded as the architect of the new power policy in 1991 which stated that no open tendering system would be employed for the frist eight 'fast track' power projects. They felt that scrapping Enron Project will scare other foreign investors from entering India. BJP + SS government had spoiled the image of India by not honouring the commitments made by the earlier democratically elected government. This issue, without any doubt, was also at stake.

Thus started a battle on all the fronts. This included press statements, pressure tactics, use of public relations which included support from the erstwhile political bosses and litigation. A considerable time elapsed before one could know whether Enron is on or not.

A division bench of the Bombay High Court in 1996 dismissed a bunch of Petitions that had challenged the legality of the beleaguered Enron power project. 'The case has highlighted to the people how even after 50 years of independence, political considerations outweight public interest and the interest of the State and to what extent the government can go to justify its actions not only before the public but even before the courts of law' were the severe words indicting the opportunistic policies of the SS + BJP government in Maharashtra.

Bouncing back of Enron

Thus, the way has been cleared to restract the work that was stalled for over eighteen months. The delays have escalated the cost by nearly $ 160 million (around Rs. 575 crore which Enron says they will absorb). The capital cost of Phase I of the 2450 MW project was estimated to be $ 920 million, but thanks to delay, it may now be in this region of $ 1.08 billion. Enron says that it is compensating the cost escalation by lowering its internal rate of return from the earlier 21 to 18%. The new deal will look as follows :

The new deal

Before Cancellation		Now
Generation of PowerPh.I 695 MW		Ph. I 826 MW
Phase II 1320 MW	Phase II 1624 MW	
Total 2015 MW		Total 2450 MW
Cost of Project Ph. I $ 920 mill.		Ph,I $ 1060 mill.
Phase II	$ 2.8 bill.	Phase II $ 2.5 bill.
Tariff	Rs. 2.40/U nit	Rs. 1.86/ KWhr
Debt (Phase I)	$ 645 million	$ 645 million
Equity (Phase I)	$ 245 million	$ 405 million

No one is sure whether Enron has been a loser in these negotiations or has actually come out a winner. Critics argue that they have on the contrary been benefitted on account of the following :

It is guaranteed to be the contractor for both the phases of the project.

The project size has been increased by more than 800 MW. It may not cost them much to expand this capacity but the benefits of selling 400 MW of additional power will be tremendous.

Experts feel that in the re-negotiated agreement, the price of power of Rs. 1.86 per Kwhr works out to much more than the Rs. 4.40 per unit that it was supposed to have charged as part of the original agreement. After all this, it is still not going to be a bed of roses for Enron. What with opposition from environmentalists like Medha Patkar and Swadeshi Jagran Manch. The latter had even threatened to take their allies BJP head on. In total volte-face, SS + BJP government appears more committed.

Issues at stake

It is, therefore, imperative to see the controversy from the perspective provided in the court order. The SS + BJP alliance could not come up with the proof whatsoever when it alleged bribery and worse in the deal. The justification to cancel the contract could not be made. Without any doubt, the entire exercise helped the alliance come to power in the state but put a big question mark over the investment prospects of Maharashtra and, indeed, the country. It is also important here to question whether in the name of ideological opposition and public interests, can activists be allowed to hold critical and crucial projects like Enron prolonged litigation tantamounting to shopping for justice. On the other hand, by refusing to go into the economic and technical viability of the project and choosing not to clearly define the role of the Central Electrical Authority, the court's order leaves room for further litigations. History will have to evaluate dispassionately and impartially the roles played by all individuals as well as organizations and their modus operandi to enter a particular country. For us, the roles played by the polity, bureaucracy, technocrats, social activists and finally by the common man, the voter, to whom all the above profess to serve. All these are the causes of consternation to decide what was ethical and what was not?

Questions :

- Discuss the ethical issues involved in business promotion? What strategies MNCs use?

- Discuss the major issues of 'Commission and Omission' in this case.

(Note: This case was used at Tata Management Training Centre (TMTC) in July 1986 for a training program organized for senior IAS officers under the instructions from Mr. Rajiv Gandhi, the then PM of India).

Priorities - Individual versus Organizational

The HOD of a certain division of TCR was a worried man. He had received a complaint about the malfunctioning of a certain product supplied to a Utility Organization based in Baroda. The product was under warrantee and the repairs had to be done on an emergency basis within 24 hours. He had a service engineer ready for the same. However, it was October 22 and Diwali vacations were there for next 3 days. The service engineer flatly refused to go. He promised to go on October 26. No amount of coaxing & coercing could work. Even a threat of serving him a memo for disciplinary action or any further punishment was of no use.

The HOD had to cut a sorry figure with the client. He had to profusely apologize. This could have resulted badly on future business.

Was this the first of its kind of experience? Or is it a recurring phenomenon at TCR?

Excusitis

The magic of thinking big is a book written by Dr. David J.Schwartz which has sold more than 4 million copies worldwide. The book is generally classified as a self help book. It is believed to be a highly effective and interesting tool that helps its readers to enhance the power of positive thinking in their daily lives.

Chapter 2 in this book talks about Cure Yourself of Excusitis, the Failure Disease. The author elaborates that most of the people come out with four major excuses to avoid work. They are,

1. Health excusitis

2. Intelligence excusitis

3. Age excusitis

4. Luck excusitis

They are not bothered that this will result in getting a bad name for them as well as for the organization. They are also not worried that this may affect their chances of promotion as well as increments when the annual appraisals will be done. Aren't executives worried about their careers?

The author of the book gives advice on overcoming these symptoms as follows:

- **Health excusitis:** Never complain about your health. You are as young as you feel.

- **Intelligence excusitis:** Never underestimate your own intelligence. Attitude is more important than intelligence. Ability to think is of more value that memorizing facts.

- **Age excusitis:** It is not the age but experience matters.

- **Luck excusitis:** Learn from the mistakes. Luck is the residue of diligence. Harder you work, luckier you get.

The question is, are these only rhetoric? How does it happen in real life?

The concerned HOD brought this point for discussion in the next weekly meeting with the CEO along with other HOD's. It was the same story with others. In last 2 months, at least 5 such similar cases were reported. They were as follows:

1. An officer talked about the health problems of his family member. Citing that his wife is a diabetic and also suffering from varicose vein and consequently needs to take care of his young son and is reluctant for outstation visits that are necessary for his functional obligation. This employee requested for a transfer to some function that does not require travel.

2. At least three members of staff from the PC function of a division comprising a total strength of four members were appearing for exams relating to the same course. All of them applied for 10 days leave for a same period. None of them thought it fit to take prior permission before joining the course. They also knew that the period of leave solicited was the peak manufacturing period and division had also to make up for earlier shortfalls in quantities.

3. A person was selected as a functional head in marketing. He was clearly told at the time of interview that this job involves travelling for at least 20 days in a month. He had accepted this condition. After 6

months, he refused to travel and made a request to his superior to transfer him to a profile that does not require travel.

4. The Company showed gratitude in reemploying a person. This employee subsequently underwent an open heart surgery. On joining after three months of sick leave with a fitness certificate was reluctant to go for outstation visits that were part of his contractual obligations. This employee also made a request to transfer him to a profile that does not require travel.

5. An employee had the audacity to fill in leave form for 10 days of Ganesh Festival, year after year, on the grounds that he was the eldest in the family and had to visit his hometown to perform puja.

6. There are others who follow a routine of eight hours work irrespective of exigencies that may demand working for little longer at times.

7. Few others may be resorting to double employment after observing eight hours of duty without keeping the Company informed. Here again functional exigencies suffer.

It became imperative to decide the HR Policy on such matters as it had a direct bearing on customer relations and eventually affecting the business. Prompt customer service can only generate confidence.

Individual priorities

It is but natural that individuals would like to decide their goals in life. They would include,

- **Career goals:** A person after completing education normally gets a span of around 35-37 years in a career. He/she can plan the career goals It can be generalized that only 10% people will be ambitious to reach the top most position. For, this they will draw a plan and work accordingly. The remaining, 90% will get promotions on time scale basis. The Peter's Principle then will be applicable, namely, everyone will reach his level of incompetency beyond which it will not matter.

- **Family goals:** This may include such issues as marriage, raising a family, careers for children and many others. There is nothing wrong if a person is attached to his family. The question will arise if he gives more priority to family than his job!

- **Financial goals:** This could include such aspects like expectations on salary, savings, investment and others. As long as these goals are achieved through honest means, no one will have any objections.

- **Goals regarding extra- curricular activities:** There is certainly life beyond work and family. A person may like to set goals on hobbies, health, social work and others aspects.

As against this, let us now look at the organizational goals.

Organizational goals

Depending on the nature of your work and the level at which you work, the goals may vary. However, all individual goals will be related to overall organizational goals. Everyone will have to work to achieve them. They will include,

- Achieving a certain revenue for a defined period

- Achieving a certain profit on the turnover

- Achieving a certain market share in the total and defined market.

- Generating 100% customer satisfaction.

- Any other

There is no reason to have any clash between the individual and organizational goals. They are mutually exclusive. The problem occurs if an individual priority of one takes over the other as we have seen in the earlier situations. And if it is at the cost of harming the interest of the organization, then solutions will have to be sought.

Work life

There are different types of jobs which are performed by individuals. They can be broadly categorized as,

a. **Field jobs:** This will include jobs in field selling, servicing of engineering goods, consumer durables and others. When one accepts this kind of job, it is well understood that it will involve considerable touring which might affect the family life. No wonder younger people before their marriage prefer this type of job. They can see the world at company's expenses; they like to travel and meet different people and also may earn more on account of field allowances and incentives given on achieving the targets.

However, this type of job can become tiresome after some time and a person may like to opt for an office job. A general belief prevails that females may not be ideally suited in this area.

b. **Office jobs:** Some people may opt for this kind of job which they may see as less tiring sitting in an air-conditioned office with much less physical strain. May be people get this with seniority?

The share of gender in our population is 52% males and 48% females. However, less than 10% of female population is working in supervisory and managerial position. IT sector is booming presently. Approximately, IT sector employees are around 30% females. As the focus of IT is mainly on exports, it creates different types of problems for professionals due to time difference in different zones. For example, the west coast in USA, typically called as silicon valley is 12 hours behind India. This may call for working in 3 shifts which may create problems for female employees.

The female employees also have to face the natural problem of motherhood. They have to go on long maternity leave. When the children are small, looking after them could be a full time job. Who will look after the children and other household chores could be a matter of conflict between the spouses. Many talented women abandoning their careers is not uncommon. There are few cases of women who decided not to have children because their career mattered more to them.

There are, of course, successful women executives who have managed to have a balanced work life. This include successful entrepreneurs, business executives, political leaders and professionals like doctors, lawyers and others.

Balancing work and home life

Whether males or females, each one will have to plan this balancing act. It is not difficult to do this without any guilt or stressing out. At the same time, individual aspirations can be fulfilled. By observing successful people who have achieved this in different walks of life can teach a lot.

Some alternatives to achieve this have been identified as follows:

a. **Joint family system:** The old joint family system is being revived. This can take care of rearing of children. Particularly, having grandparents in the house has been found to be a boon. Particularly, females give credit to their in-laws for this balancing act.

b. **Facilities of crèche:** Many working women keep their babies in the crèche. They drop them while going for work and collect while returning from work. Even many corporates have given a sympathetic view on this issue by providing crèche facilities in the office.

c. **Family outings:** This is one way of maintain a good relationship in the family. Periodic get together and outings establish a stronger bond between the members in the family. However, an amount of flexibility and understanding is needed. Sometime, it may not be possible to take off on holidays or on festive occasions. The celebrations can be done at other times.

d. **Counseling:** Family conflicts are on the rise. They could be on many accounts such as alcoholism, adultery, incompatability, schizophrenia and others. Professional help is available in the form of psychiatrists, psychologists and others in counseling. Their help can be taken to resolve the conflicts. Many corporates are employing the services of such professionals one a week or so to advise staff members.

e. **Relatives & colleagues:** These people can also chip in occasionally on a reciprocal basis. However, one will have to learn how to maintain good relationships?

Your behavior depends significantly on what environments you have been brought up, what family culture you have witnessed and your value system and beliefs. This is reflected in your behavior.

What do the counselors advice?

The counselors believe that it is possible to have a good balance between your work and family life. For this, some suggestions can be as follows:

* **Role clarity:** Be very clear about your role as a business executive as well as a family member. Understand the expectations from each job.

* **Prioritization:** It is very crucial that you are very clear on this issue. Each area needs to be attended to without compromising with other.

- **Good communication:** Clear communication with all concerned is necessary. In order to please one, bluffing the other, will certainly land you in trouble.

- **Good time management:** This ultimately is the crux in the balancing act. With experience, one will have to learn the time management which will result in win-win situation.

The CEO requested all HODs to come out with options/ alternatives which will be able to tackle such situations. They may include harsh steps like reprimands, stopping increments and promotions and even firing from the job. However, he also requested another option like counseling /motivating the subordinates. Customer service and organization reputation is of prime importance.

Give solutions to the issue and any creative ideas.

Marketing of RDC Facilities

Creation of Fixed Assets

Entrepreneurs in order to set up an enterprise have got to invest in fixed assets. Similarly, a going organization invests in fixed assets for expansion and growth. The objectives of both are common, namely,

a. To tap the market opportunities.

b. To create wealth through it by using the assets for business operations.

c. The fixed assets like land, plant & machinery, technical know-how and other sundry assets on books normally depreciate. However, in reality they appreciate thereby enhancing the wealth.

d. For creation of employment opportunities.

e. The government offers different incentives for setting up of industries particularly in backward regions and notified no industries districts. Incentives are also available to set up research & development (R & D) facilities.

TCR has set up testing facilities at Nasik. This project has been named as Research & Development

Center (RDC). The major reasons in creating these facilities are as follows:

- TCR is in business of manufacturing electrical equipments mainly tap changers, radiators and others now for over 50 years. As such, they are one of the pioneers in this line and also market leaders for some of the products. It was a natural growth strategy to create testing facilities.

- When TCR did not have their own facilities, they had to go to other existing laboratories for this purpose. While they had to pay substantial fees for getting the tests done, the major hindrance was on account of the time it used to consume. Sometimes, they had to wait for over six months to get the facilities. This resulted in delays in taping market opportunities.

The facilities installed are for the following tests:

a. Power frequency test up to 700 kVrms.

b. Impulse test up to 1800 kVp

c. Short circuit current test 10 kA for 3 Sec.

d. Temperature rise test up to 300 Amps

e. Partial discharge test up to 700 kV

f. Tan Delta test

g. Switching impulse up to 1200 kVp

h. Switching test:

I. Service duty test for Tap changers at 1500 Amps with 3800 Volts

J. Breaking capacity test at 750 Amps with 3800 Volts.

TCR has invested close to Rs.14 Crores in creating this facility. This is inclusive of building, machinery and other infrastructural inputs. The current level of revenue expenditure are to the tune of Rs.150.00 Lakhs p.a. As per present scheme of government of India, RDC is entitled to tax benefits on 200% of the revenue and capital investment. Such revenue expenditure shall be net of income from RDC. However, it must be made clear that CTR did not create these facilities only to claim the tax benefits. They would like to put the facilities to captive use as well as offer this as a service to other electrical equipment manufacturers for revenue generation and adding to its bottom line.

Earlier, only the laboratories of ERDA at Vadodara and Central Power Research Institute at Bhopal and Bangalore were available. Now CTR can match the facilities, in limited areas of testing.

Investment appraisal

It is a natural expectation that the investments made should fulfill the objectives. For all business organizations, profit undoubtedly is a major objective.

There are three standard procedures used to appraise the investments made. They are discussed briefly here.

1. Return on investment method

The Profit & loss projections made over the years estimate the likely profit. Then considering the project life, it can be estimated as to how much returns are made on the total capital employed over the period. This ratio is call ROCE. Similarly ROE (Return on equity) can also be calculated when an organization is considering two different projects, then this method helps in selecting the project which gives a higher ROCE,

An illustration with hypothetical figures is given below:

- Average investment   Rs.50,000
- Project life   10 years
- Profit during project life   Rs.30,000
- Annual return   Rs.3000
- Return on investment   6%

2. Cash flow method

Many times, the profit projections do not materialize due to conditions beyond control. Another method used for investment appraisal projects the likely cash flow over the span of the project. When two projects are under consideration, the project which results in higher cash flow is selected.

An illustration with hypothetical figures is given below:

Investment   **Rs.10,000**

Net Cash flows

- First year   3000
- Second year   3000
- Third year   4000

- Fourth year   3000
- Fifth year   2000
- **Payback period**   3 years

Thus, it can be seen that the original investment is recovered within three years.

3. Net present value or discounted cash flow method

It is a fact that the value of currency declines every year due to inflation. Hence, when the life of the equipment is over, in order to replenish it, a higher amount is required than the one which was invested at the beginning of the project. The amount is getting discounted over the years. This method then tells us how much should be the cash generation considering the decline of the currency.

An illustration with hypothetical figures is given below:

- **Investment**   **Rs.40,000**

- **Estimated cash flows (Years/Rupees)**

I year	10,000
II year	12,000
III year	15,000
IV year	12,000
V year	10,000
VI year	5,000

- **Total for 6 years**   **64,000**

Discounted cash flow

Year	Disc. Factor (16%)	
1.	0.862	8620
2.	0.743	8916
3.	0.641	9615
4.	0.552	6624
5.	0.476	4760
6.	0.410	2050
Total		**40.585**
Less original investment		0,000
Net present value		(+)585

Thus, it can be seen that using discounted cash flow, over the period; it results in a positive cash flow considering a certain discounting factor.

Facilities available at RDC

Presently, impulse and power frequency tests up to 75 MVA of transformers are offered. The balance test facilities as cited earlier herein will be operational by July 2015. The present manpower at RDC is 22 which will increase as the need arises.

Marketing of RDC

Whether it is marketing of a product like tap changer or services like RDC, the approach to marketing will remain same. Given below are some of the steps that will have to be carried out to market RDC.

a. **Market research:** A limited primary market research can be conducted to identify target customers. Depending on resources available, the market research can be done through a postal or e-mail survey or by personally visiting the potential customers and understanding their requirements.

b. **Creation of a data base:** A data base can be created of potential customers for RDC. They can be categorized as A class customers who will be large manufacturers or utilities needing services more frequently. B class customers who could be casual customers and C class customers who may use the facilities occasionally.

c. **Creating awareness:** A communication campaign can be started to create awareness of RDC. This may include direct mailers with a covering letter and a brochure on RDC to inviting A class customers to visit the facilities and witnessing some tests.

d. **Designing a price structure:** A price list can be prepared for various tests can be conducted at RDC. An incentive can be offered for large customers who will use the facilities more than others.

e. **Annual target:** Based on the market research and the feedback obtained, an estimate can be made on the total potential available. From this, annual target can be set up for revenue generation.

f. **Monitoring and control:** A time table can be prepared for conducting the tests and delivering the reports. Strict adherence to the same will enhance the credibility.

g. RDC will be offering intangibles. If TCR can maintain quality norms and fulfill the expectations of customers, it will become popular.

The questions that arise are:

1. Should we extend the scope of our revenue by being a service provider using RDC facilities other than for captive use?

2. Apart from captive use TCR will be able to spare 200 days of capacity. Identify prospective service recipients? Should we consider competitors products in to this?

3. What would be the marketing strategy and pricing methodology?

4. If the answer to the above is in the affirmative, can RDC turn out to be a profit centre?

5. If the answer is in the negative, can RDC survive as a Cost Centre exclusively on tax benefits which is subject to renewal of accreditation by DSIR every 3 years and the changing government policies.

6. Should we view ROCE on the amount invested or on the quantum of such investments net of tax concessions?

Offer your suggestions on how the RDC can be made successful so that it enhances the image of TCR and also adds to its top and bottom lines?

www.ingramcontent.com/pod-product-compliance
Lightning Source LLC
Chambersburg PA
CBHW021925190326
41519CB00009B/915